D1006282

PREPARE
HIM
ROOM

BOOKS BY SUSIE LARSON

A DAILY ADVENT DEVOTIONAL

PREPARE HIM ROOM

SUSIE LARSON

BETHANY HOUSE
a division of Baker Publishing Group
Minneapolis, Minnesota

Published by Bethany House Publishers
11400 Hampshire Avenue South
Bloomington, Minnesota 55438
www.bethanyhouse.com

Bethany House Publishers is a division of
Baker Publishing Group, Grand Rapids, Michigan

Printed in China

ISBN 978-0-7642-3807-9 (cloth)
ISBN 978-1-4934-3356-8 (ebook)

Cover design by Brand Navigation

Author is represented by The Steve Laube Agency.

21 22 23 24 25 26 27   7 6 5 4 3 2 1

To Mom
For making Christmastime something to behold.
Love you so much,
Susie

CONTENTS

Contents

AUTHOR'S NOTE

I've been a big proponent of fasting for many years. I don't believe fasting needs to be limited to food. (Some people have health issues that keep them from entering a standard fast.) I've done creative fasts for decades (social media, TV, sweet treats, snacks, etc.). My husband, Kev, and I recently read Dr. Alicia Britt Chole's book *40 Days of Decrease*, in which she invites the reader to a different fast each day (fast from skepticism, self-protection, etc.). The fasts at the end of each chapter in this Advent devotional were inspired both by Dr. Chole's book and my own passion to practice restraint in seasons of indulgence. I highly recommend Dr. Chole's book for your Lenten season. It's a brilliant read. I pray you'll enter this journey with your whole heart.

INTRODUCTION

PREPARE: *To make ready; to make necessary adjustments; to position yourself to receive your King and to receive His blessing.*

Christmas is a time of great joy, expectancy, and celebration. Yet all too often we lose ourselves in holiday preparations and miss the sacredness of the season. Why does it matter? Because it's *this* holiday on which we honor the birth of our Savior. It's *this* time of year when people are most open to the things of God. And it's precisely *this* season when Christians most often lose sight of what's available to them in Christ Jesus.

We are people created in God's image. We have access to His presence and His promises. So why all the strain and stress? Dare we ask ourselves what honestly matters most to us this season?

God invites us to push away the clutter, turn down the noise, and offer Him the sacred space in our lives so that the King of Glory may enter, take up residence, and radically change us from the inside out. We can race through the holiday season more stressed than blessed, or we can slow down, ponder the reality of Christ within us, and *respond* to His miraculous work within us.

Change your focus, determine your pace, adjust your priorities, and this could be your most life-giving holiday season yet.

Change your focus, determine your pace, adjust your priorities, and this could be your most life-giving holiday season yet.

Whether you already walk intimately with Jesus or you see Him more like a distant relative, do know He's very near and that He came to redeem every aspect of who you are.

The gospel of Luke offers us a detailed account of Jesus' birth, life, death, and ultimate resurrection. Jesus' life will transform ours if we let Him. Journey with me through this amazing gospel. Let's prepare our hearts to encounter Jesus in a fresh, compelling, and life-changing way.

Let earth receive her King!

> *With breathless expectancy,*
> *Susie Larson*

Day 1

EMBRACE EXPECTANCY

Today's Reading: Luke 1

OTHER PASSAGES TO PONDER

But if we look forward to something we don't yet have, we must wait patiently and confidently. —Romans 8:25

In the morning, O Eternal One, listen for my voice;
in the day's first light, I will offer my prayer to You and
watch expectantly for Your answer. —Psalm 5:3 VOICE

*The message of Christmas . . . is not about manufacturing senti-
mental feelings in vain hopes of a miracle. It's about believing the
reality that God has birthed something new in Jesus and because
of this, God will birth something new in you and in me. And that*

newness is breaking out, still today, in the hearts of God's people amidst a broken world. —*Daniel Darling*[1]

Something new. When it comes to the lives and hearts of God's people, God is always up to something new. Though we love to look for signs or subtle shifts in circumstance, though it's such a gift to sense God's presence and receive insight from His Word, He's working even when we can't see Him, feel Him, or sense Him. He's always working, continually listening to our prayers and faithfully interceding for us—orchestrating circumstances that, when displayed in all their fullness, will reveal God's fatherly heart for His children, will unveil His meticulous attention to detail, and will leave us breathless.

All of heaven is *for* us. Imagine.

What joy when the breakthrough finally comes! What a blessing when He reminds us that He keeps His promises.

Yet how do we navigate *before* the breakthrough comes? What are we to do with our disappointments? How are we to frame our heartbreaks in light of God's promises?

———

Righteous and barren. Honorable and heartbroken. It's hard to put such words together.

Zechariah and Elizabeth were righteous in God's eyes, careful to obey all of the Lord's commandments and regulations.

They had no children because Elizabeth was unable to conceive, and they were both very old.

Luke 1:6–7

Zechariah and Elizabeth loved God and honored Him with their lives, even though their quiet home reminded them daily that God hadn't come through for them in the way they had hoped.

What happens in your heart when God doesn't give you what you want? Do you loosen your grip on what you know to be true? Do you wander from the very things that keep your soul free and whole? Especially at Christmastime, we tend to gravitate toward indulgence because we prefer to feel a surface level of happiness rather than to acknowledge the pain buried beneath the surface.

But the loving voice of our Savior beckons us back to honesty so He can lead us to a better place of hopeful expectancy. He never overlooks our prayers or underestimates our worth. He delights in every detail of our lives. Confident hope is our birthright when we belong to Him.

Elizabeth and Zechariah were people of depth and conviction. They honored God with their lives even though (it seemed) He hadn't heard their prayer.

But then one day their story took a turn. And, *as it happened* . . . Don't you just love that phrase? I would like to study every "as it happened" moment in Scripture. I wonder if I'd find stories of God's people faithfully tending to their

God-given duties, unsuspecting of the sudden shift in the spiritual atmosphere.

God ordained it one day for Zechariah to enter the Temple to offer sacrifices. I'm not sure what Zechariah expected, but I think it's safe to say he was not at all prepared for what was about to happen. Zechariah was alone. And then he wasn't. Right before his eyes an angel of the Lord visibly appeared and spoke audibly to Zechariah. Not a dream or vision. This happened!

Try to imagine Zechariah's response. His cheeks flushed, his heart raced, and he forgot to breathe. Zechariah was shaken to his core and overwhelmed with fear. Think about it. Even though Zechariah righteously loved and honored God, he was speechless when God finally moved miraculously in his life.

I wish I could have overheard Zechariah's prayers when he wasn't at the temple, could have seen how he turned his eyes upward from time to time. Zechariah kept his heart engaged with the things of God. That's a big deal when your story hasn't turned out as you'd hoped.

> While Zechariah was in the sanctuary, an angel of the Lord appeared to him, standing to the right of the incense altar. Zechariah was shaken and overwhelmed with fear when he saw him. But the angel said, "Don't be afraid, Zechariah! God has heard your prayer. Your wife, Elizabeth, will give you a son, and you are to name him John. You will have great joy and gladness, and many will rejoice at his birth."
>
> Luke 1:11–14

The angel Gabriel not only announced the promise that this dear couple would have a son, but that this boy would be great in the eyes of God, filled with the Holy Spirit even before his birth! Marked by the spirit and power of Elijah, John would prepare the way for the coming of the Lord. John's holy influence would turn the hearts of fathers to their children. Imagine. His humble, holy presence on the earth would cause the rebellious to accept the wisdom of the godly.

Even though God delays, He delivers.

The Lord then sent Gabriel on another assignment: to Nazareth. Gabriel appeared before Mary and called her highly favored of God. He announced that she would give birth to a son, the Son of the Most High God.

> The angel replied, "The Holy Spirit will come upon you, and the power of the Most High will overshadow you. So the baby to be born will be holy, and he will be called the Son of God. What's more, your relative Elizabeth has become pregnant in her old age! People used to say she was barren, but she has conceived a son and is now in her sixth month. For the word of God will never fail."
>
> Luke 1:35–37

People used to say Elizabeth was barren. But no more.

Do you believe God is capable of changing the narrative of your story? Can you embrace the idea that He wants to do such a thing for you?

What if you engaged your faith this Advent season? Decided to believe for the impossible? Prioritized things you know are necessary? And what if you dared to lift your requests before the Lord? Are you ready to dream again? It's time for expectancy to make a comeback.

Step out of the hustle-bustle of the season. Find a quiet place to rest and reflect. What comes to the surface for you? How have your delays impacted you? Are you mad? Sad? Expectant and glad? Most of us tend to loosen our grip when we lose heart, yet this is precisely the time to lean in and engage your faith and dare to believe once more. It takes great maturity to embrace holy contentment and holy expectancy simultaneously. Great things happen in the heart of one who holds fast to faith, peace, and gratitude, all mixed with an essential dose of expectant hope.

> *It takes great maturity to embrace holy contentment and holy expectancy simultaneously.*

Though God often answers our prayers in ways different than we ever expect, He will answer. He's Emmanuel.

God is *with you*. Go about your daily duties with a renewed awareness of God's presence. Be joyful. And thankful. Embrace expectancy. And when God moves in and upon your circumstances, dare to pray what Mary prayed:

Mary responded, "I am the Lord's servant. May everything you have said about me come true."

Luke 1:38

Prepare Him Room

Lord, I am Your servant. May everything You've said about me come true. May everything You want for me become my reality. Show me my self-limiting thoughts. Reveal to me my own God-limiting beliefs. Nothing is too complicated for You! I don't want a rat-race holiday. I want to be present with You this Christmas season. I will look for You. I'll listen to You. I'll live with expectancy because of You. O come, Thou long-expected Savior. My soul waits for You. Amen.

Look Up

Fast from impatience and discontentment. Pursue God until you come to a place of holy contentment mixed with holy expectancy. His grace abounds for you here.

Day 2

THE SAVIOR OF THE WORLD

Today's Reading: Luke 2

OTHER PASSAGES TO PONDER

Therefore, since we have been made right in God's sight by faith, we have peace with God because of what Jesus Christ our Lord has done for us. Because of our faith, Christ has brought us into this place of undeserved privilege where we now stand, and we confidently and joyfully look forward to sharing God's glory. —Romans 5:1–2

God saved you by his grace when you believed. And you can't take credit for this; it is a gift from God. Salvation is not a reward for the good things we have done, so none of us can boast about it. For we are God's masterpiece. He has created us anew in Christ Jesus, so we can do the good things he planned for us long ago. —Ephesians 2:8–10

The entire universe worships the King of kings—but as humans, we often miss out on this privilege. We're often so focused on ourselves that we become prideful, angry, and annoyed with others, especially in the busyness of the holiday season. Today, take your eyes off yourself, and fix your gaze on the King of Glory. Worship Him today. —Asheritah Ciuciu[1]

Over two thousand years ago, shepherds stood on a hillside as they had done countless times before. They were most likely guarding sheep that would later serve as a sacrifice at the temple. Imagine what a night's work might look like for them. The stars overhead, the moon shining brightly; animal noises fill the air as the shepherds banter back and forth. Here again, you find unsuspecting souls going about their daily duties, unaware that heaven is about to invade earth.

That night there were shepherds staying in the fields nearby, guarding their flocks of sheep. Suddenly, an angel of the Lord appeared among them, and the radiance of the Lord's glory surrounded them. They were terrified, but the angel reassured them. "Don't be afraid!" he said. "I bring you good news that will bring great joy to all people. The Savior—yes, the Messiah, the Lord—has been born today in Bethlehem, the city of David! And you will recognize him by this sign: You will find a baby wrapped snugly in strips of cloth, lying in a manger."

Suddenly, the angel was joined by a vast host of others— the armies of heaven—praising God and saying,

> "Glory to God in highest heaven,
>> and peace on earth to those with whom God is pleased."

Luke 2:8–14

The first Christmas was anything *but* commercialized, hurried, or overdone. Jesus came into the world through the womb of a poor, teenage girl, was born in a cave and placed in an animal trough. The world didn't make room for Him. Still, heaven celebrated Him. Those with ears bent toward heaven discerned Jesus' presence on the earth. The power of the Most High God rested upon this little makeshift gathering of shepherds, a baby, and His young parents. But much of the world missed Him then just as many in the world miss Him now. Yet He came to us anyway. What a gift God's given us!

Interestingly, as Jesus grew up, some recognized Him immediately because they'd been waiting for Him. Others actually observed His miracles, watched Him fulfill prophecies before their very eyes, and still refused to believe. Every heart needs Him. Few are willing to receive Him.

The Savior of the World

In her Bible study *Secrets Jesus Shared*, Jennifer Kennedy Dean writes,

> Every step that Jesus took on Planet Earth, the spiritual realm was shouting: "This is what God is like!" As He healed and taught and touched and laughed and loved, "This is what God is like!" As He hung broken on the cross, "This is what God is like!" When He rose from the grave and triumphed over death, "This is what God is like!"[2]

Have you noticed it? Celebrities, pop stars, and high-level leaders typically have an entourage to serve them, to anticipate and meet their needs. Someone to cook, clean, run errands, or run interference. Imagine what that would do to your ego if you had people to open doors, serve you food, and treat you like you're more important than they are.

Many in positions of power or prosperity leverage their privilege in a way that benefits them even if it unfairly costs another.

Before there was time, there was Jesus. Every created thing came through Him. He is the star-breathing God, the King of the universe, and the Savior of the world. Yet Jesus did not even consider equality with God something to manipulate for His benefit. He did precisely the opposite. Jesus leveraged His status as God because He could, for our benefit. And it cost Him His life.

Prideful people won't even wait on hold unless they'll be talking to someone more prideful and vital than themselves. But Jesus stands at the door of your heart and knocks. And waits. And lets you decide if you'll let Him in.[3] Asheritah Ciuciu writes,

> We do not trifle with a weakling, nor do we worship an incompetent wannabe rock star. We worship the King of kings who deserves all the honor and glory, and continually receives if from the heavens, creation, angels, and the chorus of His redeemed. Who is this King of Glory? His name is Jesus.[4]

The King of the universe is not a tyrannical leader. He's the Savior of the world. The Christmas story isn't old news. It's good news. It's *now* news! Salvation is not just an addendum to the end of your life, and Christmas isn't just a quaint little story. When Jesus was born, God's kingdom came to earth!

The Christmas story isn't old news. It's good news. It's NOW news!

Don't let another moment pass by without giving God the glory He deserves. He sent His Son to die in your place. Celebrate with joy. Give meaningful gifts to those you love. Help the poor. And enjoy a good party. But *refuse* to let the commercialism of Christmas quench the true spirit of this earth-shaking holiday. Jesus came, and He's coming again. Oh, worship the King of Glory, for He has done great things.

Prepare Him Room

Jesus, my Savior, You came! You saw a world desperately in need, and You came. I receive Your gift of grace. I believe You died in my place. Forgive me of my sins, cleanse me from all unrighteousness, fill me with the power of the Holy Spirit, and show me how to live in a manner worthy of Your name. The holidays quickly become self-indulgent noise if You're not in them. Fill my home, my family, and my heart with the wonder of Your love and presence. Amen.

Look Up

Fast today from a shallow commercialized holiday. Refuse to get weighed down by temporary circumstances. Consider the heavenly wonder that surrounds this actual celebration. Marvel that Jesus came to earth on a rescue mission with you on His mind. Rejoice!

Day 3

PREPARE THE WAY

Today's Reading: Luke 3

OTHER PASSAGES TO PONDER

Don't copy the behavior and customs of this world, but let God transform you into a new person by changing the way you think. Then you will learn to know God's will for you, which is good and pleasing and perfect. —Romans 12:2

So all of us who have had that veil removed can see and reflect the glory of the Lord. And the Lord—who is the Spirit— makes us more and more like him as we are changed into his glorious image. —2 Corinthians 3:18

Heaven is for sinners who face their sin; hell is for those who refuse to see. One of the ironic similarities between heaven and hell is that no one in either place thinks they got what they deserve. —*John Fischer* [1]

We got pregnant on our honeymoon. This twist in our story startled us. We delivered our firstborn son just days before Christmas. I nestled him close by the light of our Charlie Brown Christmas tree, and my soul flooded with delight. I gazed at a miracle in my arms. I looked around our tiny home and pondered all we needed to do to make room for our new boy. I'd do anything for this little one. Our lives would never be the same.

I was just about to write the old cliché, "No one prepared me for the journey of motherhood," but I think a more accurate statement is this: I had no idea what I was in for; the love, the worry, the fear, the heartbreaks, and the triumphs. No clue. But I wasn't ill-prepared. God used my journey *to* prepare me. Whenever we ask for more from God, He asks for more from us.

———

Then John went from place to place on both sides of the Jordan River, preaching that people should be baptized to show that they had repented of their sins and turned to God to be forgiven. Isaiah had spoken of John when he said,

"He is a voice shouting in the wilderness,
'Prepare the way for the LORD's coming! Clear the road
for him!
The valleys will be filled, and the mountains and hills
made level.
The curves will be straightened, and the rough places
made smooth.
And then all people will see the salvation sent from God.'"

Luke 3:3–6

John shouted to the crowds: "Prepare the way for the Lord!" Prepare? How? Did John expect people to rush home, get their act together, and come back another day for their baptism? What did he mean when he charged people to clear the way for Jesus?

With a booming voice and deep conviction, John urged people to acknowledge their need for a Savior, to own their sin. You'll never be free from a sin you refuse to recognize.

Ultimately, John was saying, *"Prepare to change. Don't just rush into the waters of baptism to escape hell. Acknowledge your need for a Savior. Repent of your sin. You prepare a way for the Lord in your life when you give Him room to work on you and in you—to change you from the inside out. Are you ready to turn from your selfish, sinful ways to follow Jesus on His terms? Are you ready for such a radical lifestyle change? This is not your work. You can't do this for yourself. It's the work of Christ within you—your hope of glory. Make no mistake, He will bring the high places low. He will humble you and dismantle your ego. He will lift the heavy burden from your shoulders and even carry you when you're too weary to walk on your own. He will put you right where you're thinking wrong. He'll not only save your soul, He'll transform you into someone you never dreamed you could be. But the road won't be easy; you won't feel prepared for such a journey. But Jesus will prepare you for all He has for you. Salvation is not an escape route out of hell. It's the radical redemption of your life."*

You may ask, "What should I do?" The crowds asked the same question.

God deals differently with all of us. He urged some to give out of their excess to the poor. If you have extra, give some to the poor. He told the corrupt tax collectors to quit swindling people out of their money. If you've been cheating others, you should stop doing so immediately. He charged the soldiers to quit misusing their power.

Maybe you're in a position of influence and you've leveraged your role in your favor. If so, ask God for forgiveness and begin to do the opposite. Use your power to make life better for others.

———

Christmastime probably isn't the best time to bring up Sodom's sins, but I can't help myself. Though most of us know the city of Sodom for her sexual immorality, Scripture records it this way:

> Now this was the sin of your sister Sodom: She and her daughters were arrogant, overfed and unconcerned; they did not help the poor and needy.
>
> Ezekiel 16:49 NIV

Wow. Arrogant, overfed, and unconcerned while the poor and needy suffered outside Sodom's door. Another translation lists her sins as *pride*, *gluttony*, and *apathy*. Easy to judge such a wicked city, right? But if I'm honest, I've overthought about myself or not thought enough of others too many times to count. I've indulged in more than I needed and turned a blind eye on a need that was well within my reach to meet. God have mercy. I don't want to live that way.

Jesus *made room* for us in His heart, in His family, and at His table. He's gone away to prepare a spectacular place for us that no mind can imagine! He makes room for us every day by putting His time, energy, and attention into our lives.

How might we do the same for Him? We prepare Him room. We give Him time and space to speak to us about our lives—to correct and direct, to guide and provide.

He's a gracious, loving, giving God. In Christ Jesus, we are uncondemnable. Our sin will never condemn us! Read this powerful passage:

> For by that one offering he forever made perfect those who are being made holy.
>
> Hebrews 10:14

He's made you perfect, and now He's making you holy.

Prepare Him Room

Precious Lord, You made way for me. You made room for me in Your kingdom, in Your family. I'll never comprehend such love this side of eternity. Forgive me for being so easily tempted toward pursuits that pull me away from You. I'm sorry for using Christmastime as an opportunity to impress more than bless. Yet I've come so far. I'm not who I once was. But I want a fresh vision for who I am about to become. I bow low, open my hands, and make room for You. Speak to me, Lord. Transform me beyond my dreams and change the world through me. Amen.

Look Up

Today, fast from overdoing things in any way. Refuse to overeat, overspend, or overcommit. Write down what you're fasting from, followed by a prayer inviting Jesus to make Himself known in the space you're offering Him today. Notice the ways you've already engaged with God this season, and be grateful.

Day 4

LET THE SPIRIT LEAD

Today's Reading: Luke 4

For all who are led by the Spirit of God are children of God. —Romans 8:14

So I say, let the Holy Spirit guide your lives. Then you won't be doing what your sinful nature craves. —Galatians 5:16

It seems we have two choices at Christmastime: We can postpone consequences or purposefully prepare for presence. We can over-commit and overindulge, leaving ourselves toxic and wishing we had a do-over. Or we can practice restraint so that we might hear the gentle whisper of our Savior in inexplicable ways throughout the season. We can wake up on New Year's Day sluggish and regretful, or we can exit this year and enter the next with wide-eyed expectancy. —Susie Larson

I've watched people who don't seem to struggle with their weight. I've noticed how so many of them limit their portions. They don't attack their food the way I do. They know when to walk away." My friend pondered her dependence on food. She longed to be free. Little by little, she learned to say no to herself and make herself deal with it. Not only have the pounds melted away, but I've also seen her dependency on the Lord grow. She's free in a way she's never been before.

We all default to faux comforts at times. We'd prefer to numb out rather than acknowledge the messes that lie just beneath the surface. When we live stressed throughout the year, it's natural to throw caution to the wind for five, six weeks during the holiday season. But it's *super*natural to manage your stress and arrive at the holiday season with a grounded sense of purpose and expectancy.

Even if it's been a tough year for you, consider this Advent season an opportunity to meet with God, to hear from Him, and to respond to the gentle nudges of the Holy Spirit within you. Nothing will nourish your soul like resetting your pace to match the Savior's rhythm for you. Nothing re-energizes like saying no to your flesh so you can say yes to the Holy Spirit who's ready and willing to work in you.

Jesus returned from the Jordan River full of the Holy Spirit, who led Him *right into the desert* where the devil would tempt Him. What? After such a profound encounter with His Father, God orchestrates a face-off with His enemy? Why? Some say that Jesus obediently followed the Holy Spirit into the wilderness to endure the temptations we face so that He would know what it's like for us.

Consider this Advent season an opportunity to meet with God, to hear from Him, and to respond to the gentle nudges of the Holy Spirit within you.

Jesus aligned Himself with us in every way. He endured our suffering, even the weight of our sin, without ever sinning a day in His life. Jesus faced our temptations. He knows what it is to be physically hungry and yet spiritually strong. We can too. He understands our desire to take shortcuts—to have now what God has appointed for us later. He showed us how to postpone immediate gratification so we can walk in authority, power, and credibility on the other side of our temptation.

Some say that Jesus also purposed to undo what Adam did in the garden of Eden. He needed to shut down the enemy on every front. Let's look at some ways the enemy went after Jesus so we can more easily discern what he's after in us.

Provision

In the face of Jesus' extreme physical hunger, the devil spewed, "If you are the Son of God, tell this stone to become a loaf of bread" (Luke 4:3).

When we're hungry or in need of a physical break, we can justify almost anything. We grab for ourselves now and pay for it later. At that moment in the wilderness, Jesus was physically weak but spiritually strong. What if we interrupted our insatiable desire to overindulge, said no to ourselves, and trusted God to provide for us in a way that's *best* for us?

Might Jesus care more about your need than you do? What if He surprised you with His goodness? What if His provision strengthened your frame as well as your attachment to Him? If we don't think God cares about our hunger, we'll miss out on the beautiful experience of His provision. We'll be too full on lesser things to notice it.

Priority

It's all too easy for our priorities to get out of whack during the holiday season. What's sad is that we don't recognize how costly it can be, and this is not about following the rigid rules of religion. Not even close. It's about keeping Jesus in His rightful place in our lives. When we give priority to anything over Him, we skew our perspective, plug our ears, and miss the beautiful intimacy to which our souls are heirs.

Our hearts are at rest when Jesus is at the center. Our lives are most fruitful when we acknowledge Jesus as King. Our souls are most healthy when the Spirit leads us, even when He leads us into difficult places.

The devil tempted Jesus to take another shortcut. He offered Jesus the glory of the kingdoms of this world—far short of the glory of the New Jerusalem. Counterfeit glory now? Or divine and everlasting glory later?

> Then the devil took him up and revealed to him all the kingdoms of the world in a moment of time. "I will give you the glory of these kingdoms and authority over them," the devil said, "because they are mine to give to anyone I please. I will give it all to you if you will worship me."
>
> Luke 4:5–7

Jesus fully embraced His ultimate destiny and would not be swayed by momentary relief or the glory of mere men. He had *us* on His mind. He envisioned our eternity together and determined to persevere through to the end, knowing it would be worth it all.

Unless we have a similar sense of calling, we'll have the tendency—not only at Christmastime but all year long—to take shortcuts, posture for a position, and arrange our promotion. All of which we'll regret later, and none of which bear fruit in the long run.

Protection

When do we tempt God to cover for us? Whenever we go headlong into something without seeking Him first. Whenever we spiritualize our reckless living and think He's somehow obligated to spare us the consequences. Whenever we take liberties with our freedoms that God never intended and expect God to look the other way.

The devil knows how to use Scripture too. He twists it to fit his plan, and if we're not in step with the Holy Spirit, we'll step right into a trap meant for our harm.

> Then the devil took him to Jerusalem, to the highest point of the Temple, and said, "If you are the Son of God, jump off! For the Scriptures say,
>> 'He will order his angels to protect and guard you.
>> And they will hold you up with their hands so you
>>> won't even hurt your foot on a stone.'"
>
> Luke 4:9–11

Real protection belongs to those who abide in the shelter of God's wing. We honor Him, He shelters us. When the devil realized that he'd find no opening in Jesus' heart, he left Him for a more suitable time.

Jesus emerged from the wilderness strong and empowered by the Spirit of God, ready to declare that the kingdom had come and that captives were about to be set free.

PREPARE HIM ROOM

King Jesus, how often I miss Your best because I grab for myself. Forgive me, Lord, for filling up on lesser things that ruin my appetite for Your divine provision. I want to taste and see that You are good. I don't want to indulge in ways that dull my spiritual senses. Help me to say no to my flesh so I can more intimately experience You. Spirit of the living God, fall afresh on me this Advent season. Amen.

LOOK UP

Today, consider fasting from all media. Turn off the TV. Turn off your notifications. And put your phone down. Fill the space with either sacred quiet or worshipful music. Bend your ear toward heaven and be especially intentional about listening for God's voice.

Day 5

ADDITION, SUBTRACTION, AND MULTIPLICATION

Today's Reading: Luke 5

John answered, "It's not possible for a person to succeed— I'm talking about *eternal* success—without heaven's help. . . . That's why my cup is running over. This is the assigned moment for him to move into the center, while I slip off to the sidelines." —John 3:27, 29–30 MSG

Then he told the people to sit down on the grass. Jesus took the five loaves and two fish, looked up toward heaven, and blessed them. Then, breaking the loaves into pieces, he gave the bread to the disciples, who distributed it to the people.

They all ate as much as they wanted, and afterward, the disciples picked up twelve baskets of leftovers. About 5,000 men were fed that day, in addition to all the women and children! —Matthew 14:19–21

Off to one side sit a group of shepherds. They sit silently on the floor; perhaps perplexed, perhaps in awe, no doubt in amazement. Their night watch had been interrupted by an explosion of light from heaven and a symphony of angels. God goes to those who have time to hear him—and so on this cloudless night he went to simple shepherds. —Max Lucado[1]

We all live in the tension of the now and the not yet. Every single one of us has things we long for and dream about. And that's a good thing (most of the time). Jesus invites us to ask, seek, and knock. He teaches us to be relentless in prayer. He is, after all, the God of the impossible, the God of multiplication, and the God who makes a way where there is no way.

But sometimes we believe our dreams, accomplishments, and possessions will finally fill the void in our hearts or validate the need for acceptance in our souls. Eventually, we lay hold of some of those things and find them sorely lacking. Still, we hope, we dream, we think that one day things will be different.

But we have Jesus' presence *today*. We have access to the very throne room of heaven *today*. We're so deeply connected to the Father's heart that He delights in every single detail of our lives, even at Christmastime. Through His fatherly eyes of love, I'm sure God aches as He watches us rush to and fro like the rest of the lost world, rehearsing our way through our stressed-out task list as if we're somehow obligated to add stress and subtract rest simply because it's the holiday season.

Alan Fadling once joined me on my radio show and asked this thought-provoking question: *"If we follow an unhurried Savior, what should the pace of our lives be?"* Contrary to popular opinion, all bets aren't off during the holidays, unless you want them to be.

What if you simplified your season enough that you and your family could feel both blessed *and* at rest? What if you reduced your list of could-dos to a healthy number of should-dos and then offered them up to the one who longs to meet with you? What if you practiced some restraint in your spending? Maybe give a sacrificial gift to a family in need in your community.

The holidays will be over before you know it. But for those who walk intimately with Jesus, who follow His lead, enjoy His company, and keep His pace? For them the kingdom comes.

One day while Jesus preached on the shores of Galilee, great crowds pressed in on Him to listen to the word of God. Jesus noticed two empty boats at the water's edge. One boat belonged to Peter. Jesus stepped into the boat, and they pushed out into the water. Once Jesus had finished speaking, He told Peter, "Now go out where it is deeper and let down your nets to catch some fish."[2]

Peter was a seasoned fisherman. He knew the drill. But he was getting to know Jesus and learning to trust Him. Peter replied to the Lord, "We worked hard all last night and didn't catch a thing, but if you say so, I'll let the nets down again." Imagine the scene. Peter's got a five-o'clock shadow. He probably smells. He's tired. He's already gone through the motions too many times to count. But with Jesus, subtraction precedes multiplication. Humility precedes honor and breakthrough.

Jesus led the disciples out to the deep and asked Peter to try again. So Peter humbly took a deep breath, exhaled, and tried again. *This time* their nets were so full of fish, the fishermen's nets began to tear. They weren't prepared for such a catch!

I'm not much of a cook, but I know there's a process called reduction whereby you thicken and intensify the flavor of something by allowing it to simmer or boil. You may start with two cups of liquid and end up with a fourth of a cup.

Every serious Christ follower I've ever met has gone through a season or process of reduction. The not-so-serious

Christian may hop out of the pan when the temperature rises. But for those who humbly follow Jesus through those seasons of refinement, they will see God do a miraculous work in and through them.

Trust Jesus even though He reduces you. Understand that He is in the process of increasing you, of adding to your spiritual credibility and multiplying your impact on the world.

Notice that the fishermen caught so many fish that their trusty nets tore! Stress is part of growth; it's part of the multiplication process. When God grows you and increases your influence, you will feel stretched beyond your ability. But God is with you!

What to do? Look at what Peter did. He called in reinforcements. God designed us to make this journey alongside others. We'll never become all we can be apart from deep, abiding friendships with others. But you'll never fully realize your need for intimate friends who will shoulder your burden until you're in a position to steward a calling that's bigger than you are.

Peter was so awestruck by the catch that he was suddenly aware of his humanity. He asked Jesus to leave his presence because God's glory felt too holy for Peter's story. But Jesus knew exactly what He was doing and whom He was using. It's the same with us. When God does a new thing in us, the enemy is often right there to accuse us of our weakness, our past, and our frailties. But these are precisely why we need a Savior. Praise God. We have one!

Often, we think that when God moves us from subtraction to multiplication, we'll finally feel the validation our hearts imagine. But the converse is true. Most times, when God promotes us, new levels of insecurity arise within us. Promotions and increase don't solve anything for us in the way of identity. But they allow us to address some of the world's problems when we're willing to steward them by faith.

As we journey through this Advent season, may we remember that we live in a world of overindulgence, overcommitment, premature multiplication, and shortcuts, and shortcuts almost always lead to compromise. What if we did something otherworldly this season? What if we slowed our pace and reduced our intake? What if we instead took in the sights, the scents, and decided to be fully present this season? What if we gave God time and space to speak to us about our needs, our hopes, and His intentions toward us? Now's a perfect time to ponder anew that first Jesus came as a baby but next He'll return as a King. *And He knows your name.*

There's a way to enjoy the beauty of the season and encounter the living Savior. Instead of numbing your pain and setting aside your heartbreak until after the holiday season, give your burdens to Jesus *as* you celebrate Him this Christmas. Ask Him to show you what He's subtracting from you that He may add and multiply His influence in you! Christmas is the perfect time to receive a prophetic word from the living God about your very real life. *This* is why He came. To seek and save the lost. To destroy the works of the devil.

And to transform you into someone you never dreamed you could be.

PREPARE HIM ROOM

Jesus, forgive me for resisting Your refining work in my life. You're always good; only good. I can trust You. I want to walk with You through this season. Show me what You're after in me. Remove from my life anything that hinders my progress in You. I'm made for more. I know it. Increase my capacity for You. Amen.

LOOK UP

Ask the Lord about your fast today (from worry, fear, overeating, etc.). Consider subtracting that thing from your life as a way of life. Prayerfully reflect also on what He wants you to add (worship, rest, fellowship, generosity, etc.). Now ask God what He wants to multiply (your prayers for your kids, your offering, your spiritual growth, your insight, your faith, etc.). Write down your thoughts along with a prayer, inviting God to do a great work of subtraction, addition, and multiplication in your life.

Day 6

THE KINGDOM IS YOURS

Today's Reading: Luke 6

OTHER PASSAGES TO PONDER

But Jesus called them together and said, "You know that the rulers in this world lord it over their people, and officials flaunt their authority over those under them. But among you it will be different. Whoever wants to be a leader among you must be your servant, and whoever wants to be first among you must become your slave." —Matthew 20:25–27

For the highest God above,
  who is and always will be, the only One who is holy
    has this to say:

Eternal One: I live in the high and holy place, yet I am
with the low, the weak, and the humble.
I renew their vitality and revive their strength.
—Isaiah 57:15 VOICE

*To say that the kingdom of God is "at hand," to pray that the king-
dom of God come "on earth as it is in heaven," isn't simply to call
for new beliefs and new behaviors. It's to say that when the stone
rolled away from the tomb and Jesus emerged from within, the
upside-down world turned right-side up. Kingdom prayers shake the
pews.* AND *kingdom lives shake the earth. —Jen Pollock Michel*[1]

The Pharisees had turned the God-given law into a stale
set of talking points. They cared more about their rules
than the people entrusted to them. Self-proclaimed experts,
they confronted Jesus one day because His hungry disciples
dared to pick heads of grain to eat on the Sabbath. His response? *"Have you not read the Scriptures?"* In other words,
*"Don't you know the Torah, or, more importantly, the one who
breathed words intended to point you to Me?"* I love Jesus.

On another Sabbath day, Jesus healed a man even though
He knew the scribes and Pharisees watched Him with mali-
cious intent. Picture Jesus at that moment. He didn't shrink
back. He didn't cower. He called the man to the front of the
room. He paused and looked past him into each set of accusing

eyes, no doubt with fire, confidence, and love. Then Jesus said to the man, "Stretch out your hand," and He healed him. Jesus is the epitome of strength, compassion, and conviction.

———————

Christmas traditions can add such richness to our holiday seasons. But when we idolize traditions at the expense of those entrusted to our care, we become a little like the Pharisees and need a fresh encounter with the one who gives life and breath to every living thing.[2] The Pharisees had developed expectations around their interpretations. We too develop expectations at Christmastime because of our interpretations of what a festive holiday should look like. This isn't about semantics. It's the difference between fighting for our way and finding the Jesus way.

After Jesus' confrontation with the Pharisees, He stole away for a while to spend time with His Father. He then chose His disciples and came down to a level place where a vast multitude waited to hear what He had to say. Once again, Jesus turned their expectations upside down and showed them the way to real power, life, and kingdom love.

> And looking toward His disciples, He began speaking: "Blessed [spiritually prosperous, happy, to be admired] are you who are poor [in spirit, those devoid of spiritual arrogance, those who regard themselves as insignificant], for the kingdom of God is yours [both now and forever]. Blessed [joyful, nourished by

God's goodness] are you who hunger now [for righteousness, actively seeking right standing with God], for you will be [completely] satisfied. Blessed [forgiven, refreshed by God's grace] are you who weep now [over your sins and repent], for you will laugh [when the burden of sin is lifted]."

Luke 6:20–21 AMP

In Jesus' day, ego was king. It was a sign of virtue. Then comes the King of the new and everlasting kingdom. He models humility. He teaches love. He leads by example. In His Sermon on the Mount, Jesus dismantles worldly ways and offers an otherworldly way to live. Look at what the masses do, and you can almost always assume Jesus would do the opposite.

Have you noticed it? Expectations and entitlement reek of pride and self-indulgence. In this passage, Jesus calls you supremely blessed and much to be admired when you know where you'd be without Him. To be poor in spirit is to know your limits and understand your needs. We're all desperate for more of Jesus; we just don't all know it yet. One day we will.

When you come to the edges of yourself and your self-life shows (grumpy, grabby, etc.), don't come under condemnation (there's no condemnation if you're in Christ Jesus[3]). Instead, come to Jesus. Admit where you've fallen or failed. Confess your need. Ask for His grace and forgiveness. Then rise with great joy. You're to be admired! When you finally learn your limits, you're finally positioned to inherit more of the kingdom, of which there are no limits.

As Christ followers, we serve in a right-side-up kingdom, but we're living in an upside-down world. Read Jesus' words in this sermon. Self-indulgent laughter (picture the overfed, overindulged laughing at another's expense) will end. Their season of sin will turn on its head. But for those who've battled in the shadows, who've mourned over their sin and the sin of their land, and who've offered sacrifices of praise that cost them dearly? Well, their sacrifices of praise will become banquets of thanksgiving. That day *is* coming.

Giving gifts to the already rich is, well, fine. But offering gifts to those who cannot repay you is sacred. Want to turn this Christmas right-side-up? Give generously and thoughtfully to someone who doesn't expect a gift from you. Give another such gift to someone who's not been kind to you. Surprise them with the goodness of God. He is kind to both the ungrateful and the wicked.[4]

When humble awe and wonder replace arrogance and entitlement, *the kingdom is yours*. When you feel sorry for your sin without crumbling under a heap of despair or condemnation but instead rise with a new joy in your salvation, *the kingdom is yours*. When you ponder God's kindness to you and then extend that same grace to those who seem least deserving, *the kingdom is yours*.

Jesus reminds us at the end of this sermon that a tree is known by its fruit. What's in our lives hangs on our tree. May the kingdom of God come to your home this holiday season.

PREPARE HIM ROOM

Mighty Savior, Redeemer, and Friend, how do I ever thank You enough, let alone comprehend all You won for me? I fall to my knees, open my hands, and look up with fresh awe and wonder. You saved me. You love me. I belong to You. I'm no longer my own. Help me break free from rigid religion and stale traditions that keep me from offering life to those in need. This season is about Your kingdom for Your glory. I put it all on the table for You. Show me Your way this season. I'm all in. Amen.

LOOK UP

Fast from self-contempt today. Refuse to get stuck on your limits. Next, identify an unlikely someone and give them a generous, thoughtful gift. Someone who most likely cannot return the favor. Someone who will be surprised by your generosity.

Day 7

Encountering Jesus

Today's Reading: Luke 7

Other Passages to Ponder

For a child is born to us, a son is given to us.
    The government will rest on his shoulders.
    And he will be called: Wonderful Counselor,
    Mighty God,
Everlasting Father, Prince of Peace. —Isaiah 9:6

Taste and see that the Lord is good.
    Oh, the joys of those who take refuge in him!
    —Psalm 34:8

Maybe this is the year to see through the polished-up holiday veneer and remember the promise of Isaiah. Christ has come . . . to our crisis, our calamity, and our Christmas. He comes with good news of great joy that will bring gifts of hope and gladness as we unwrap them. He is here for you. Receive Him. —Bo Stern[1]

Yesterday we watched Jesus face off with the religious leaders. They hated Him for breaking the Sabbath just to help others. It's always about people for Jesus. Don't you just love Him? We paused and pondered His words as He delivered the famous Sermon on the Mount. We marveled as He showed us what the kingdom is really like. Those who mourn will rejoice. Those who know their need and cry out to God will experience more of Him. Those who endure for His sake will be rewarded beyond their wildest dreams. Life is hard here. But the kingdom has come and is coming. For the believer, life on earth is as hard as it gets. It only gets better from here.

Today, let's make a note of Jesus' compassion and presence in times of need. As soon as He arrived in Capernaum, Jesus encountered a group of respected Jewish elders; what a surprise to hear them plead on behalf of a Roman officer. The Jewish people were generally at odds with the Roman government officials. But this particular officer advocated for them. He spent his own money to build them a synagogue. He had a tender place in his heart for God's people. A tender spot in his heart for God too, it seemed.

The officer's slave—who meant the world to him—was sick and on the verge of dying. But before Jesus even arrived, the Roman officer sent a surprising message that revealed his discernment, humility, and faith. He believed that the one who was on His way could change things in a moment. The officer felt unworthy of having Jesus under his roof. The officer, more than others, somehow grasped Jesus' majesty and holiness. He knew enough to be undone by the presence of the living God.

This officer also understood power and delegated influence. He had leaders above him to whom he was accountable. And he was in charge of one hundred soldiers. He understood the significance of authority and knew Jesus possessed it in abundance. Jesus didn't need to take another step toward this officer's home. He could just say the word from where He stood, and the slave would be healed. And he was. Humility and faith is an irresistible combination to Jesus.

Humility and faith is an irresistible combination to Jesus.

Soon after, Jesus went to another village, and a large crowd followed Him. He came upon a funeral. This dear woman had already lost her husband and was now about to bury her only son. In those days, a woman without a man was especially vulnerable to unspeakable injustices and hardship. With her face in her hands, she wept as she dragged her feet along the dirt path. Her life as she knew it was over.

Never in a million years did she expect to encounter the Savior at the worst moment of her life. But she did, and Jesus restored her son and her life back to her that day.

> Great fear swept the crowd, and they praised God, saying, "A mighty prophet has risen among us," and "God has visited his people today." And the news about Jesus spread throughout Judea and the surrounding countryside.
>
> Luke 7:16–17

Not everyone who encountered Jesus appreciated it. Tomorrow we'll work our way through Luke 8; we'll watch Jesus miraculously restore a man to his right mind. And the community's response? They begged Him . . . *to leave.*

Jesus offended people with His steadfast commitment to His purpose—to seek and save the lost. He infuriated "respected" leaders with His willingness to dine with those they deemed scum. He unnerved many others by His utter refusal to occupy and overthrow Rome. But it was the *world* He came to save.

If we want Jesus to squish into one of the corners of our lives, we must know that He won't. If we're looking for Him to approve of everything we do and turn a blind eye to the things we should do but don't, He won't. This begs an honest question: *Do we really want to invite Jesus into the center of our lives? Do we dare give Him the space He deserves? Are we willing to acknowledge Him as our King?*

When Jesus becomes our Savior, He becomes our King. We're miraculously grafted into His royal family line. He becomes our Counselor and Friend. He secures a place for us at the marriage supper of the Lamb.[2] He defends and delivers us when the enemy presses in against us. He continually directs us in the way we should go. He forgives us of our sins and restores us from the inside out. He meets us on our dirt roads of mourning and brings life in ways we never dreamed possible. He ministers to us in our sadness and smiles with us in our gladness. Jesus is a friend of sinners. He's the Savior of the world. What a priceless gift He offers to the willing and receptive heart!

Want to encounter Jesus this holiday season? Invite Him to your party. Give Him your burdens. Trust Him with your fears. Obey Him when it doesn't suit you. Offer Him room, time, and space to rearrange your priorities and renew your perspective.

He's still a miracle-working God. His compassions will never fail. We follow Him on His terms because He knows what we cannot know this side of heaven. So we trust Him. And enjoy Him. And we celebrate the fact that by some divine miracle, we know and are intimately known by the one who put the stars in place.

I always imagined that if everyone knew how much God loves them, everyone would love Him in return. But I know that's not the case. Not everyone wants to surrender to Jesus' lordship. Not all are interested in dying to themselves that they might more boldly live for Christ. And so we pray:

Lord, open the blind eyes to the wonder of Your love! Help those who would love You if they knew You to find You this season. May they see You for who You are!

Dr. Alicia Britt Chole conveys God's passion and heart for us beautifully here:

> Through Jesus, we inherit this trio of God's Fatherhood, love, and acceptance. We inherit the affirmation from above, for God is still shouting these words of love over his children even before we are recognized or celebrated, before we make the grade or make the news or even make dinner. Before we get that promotion or even get out of bed, Father God is already shouting. Not because of any stunning accomplishment, but because of who we are through Jesus, we are his! Is there anything else in the whole wide world that our souls need to hear?[3]

To know this love changes everything. Yet Jesus forces the kingdom on no one. He wins us one at a time, by His love. We choose to follow Him and trust Him. Or not. Nobody is opted into the kingdom by way of denomination, family association, or otherwise. Jesus offers us each a gift—an unbelievable, unfathomable, life-altering gift. He not only offers us His presence, He offers us His very life. If you've not yet trusted Christ as your Savior, trust Him today.

May God's kingdom come to you, your family, and your friends this season. May the Holy Spirit stir up a hunger and thirst to know Jesus for who He is. May Christmas miracles abound for you this year.

Prepare Him Room

Jesus, King of heaven, I bow before You this day. I open my hands and look to You. Awaken my heart and soul. Show me what hinders me from knowing You in a way that changes me. I'm so grateful that You're not afraid of my messes or swayed by others' opinions. You're committed to me. You died for me. And You love me. May my whole life be an offering to You. Shine brightly through me this season. I love You. Amen.

Look Up

Today, fast from forgetfulness. Don't forget to remember the times God has come through for you. Remember His goodness. Rehearse His kindness. Know and believe that He's working in your midst even now. Keep your eyes and ears open for even the slightest evidence of God's influence in and around you. Smile and whisper a prayer of thanks. He's Emmanuel—God with us.

THE GIFT OF PRESENCE AND LISTENING

Today's Reading: Luke 8

OTHER PASSAGES TO PONDER

"Anyone with ears to hear should listen and understand." Then he added, "Pay close attention to what you hear. The closer you listen, the more understanding you will be given— and you will receive even more. To those who listen to my teaching, more understanding will be given. But for those who are not listening, even what little understanding they have will be taken away from them." —Mark 4:23–25

And so I walk in the LORD's presence as I live here on earth! —Psalm 116:9

If you aren't willing to listen to EVERYTHING *God has to say, you eventually won't hear* ANYTHING *He has to say. If you want to hear His comforting voice, you have to listen to His convicting voice. And it's often what we want to hear the* LEAST *that we need to hear* MOST. *Trust me, though, you want to hear what He has to say.* —Mark Batterson[1]

Consider the number of times throughout the gospels that Jesus said one thing and the disciples heard another. How many times did Jesus need to say, "I've been with you all this time and still you don't know? Have I not told you?" Jesus never minced words and never wasted words. His prophetic presence changed the atmosphere and continues to change the world even though scores of people missed Him then and miss Him now.

Jesus knew that many of His insights would become clear to the first-century disciples in hindsight. Still, He paused for a moment to teach the followers about the power of receptivity. He used the parable of the soils to explain the condition of our hearts and lives. He supplies potent, powerful seed, able to produce ONE HUNDRED TIMES what's planted. It's up to us to offer available, pure, receptive hearts. We're called to cultivate an atmosphere of growth in our lives so they'll explode with an abundance of fruit and life and power.

Let's look at the four soils and what we can learn from them today.

One day Jesus told a story in the form of a parable to a large crowd that had gathered from many towns to hear him: "A farmer went out to plant his seed. As he scattered it across his field, some seed fell on a footpath, where it was stepped on, and the birds ate it. Other seed fell among rocks. It began to grow, but the plant soon wilted and died for lack of moisture. Other seed fell among thorns that grew up with it and choked out the tender plants. Still other seed fell on fertile soil. This seed grew and produced a crop that was a hundred times as much as had been planted!" When he had said this, he called out, "Anyone with ears to hear should listen and understand."

Luke 8:4–8

The first three soils represent hearts that are

- not guarded,
- not grounded, and
- not given to the things of God.

What we repeatedly sow into our hearts all year long spills out of our lives when the stresses of the holidays push us around. Let's consider these soils in light of the Christmas holiday. What might it look like for the unguarded heart when Jesus comes on the scene?

Not Guarded

Picture Jesus in all His glory, strength, and wisdom. Imagine His gentle yet firm and confident demeanor. He stands in a woman's kitchen and whispers truth to her soul. But she's filled her heart with so much angst toward others that she can't hear a thing. She constantly rehashes her hurts and stirs herself right into a self-justified tizzy. God whispers to her heart, invites her to rehearse His promises instead. She senses a small opening to think differently, to believe the best, and to consider forgiveness as an option. But just as quickly, she brushes away the idea. She goes about her stressed holiday, hoping by some random chance things will be different this year.

Not Grounded

Next Jesus visits an eager soul who is always into the next new thing. She agrees to go to church with her neighbor and absolutely loves the worship and the message. She thinks to herself, *I'm going to start attending church. This is great*. But as soon as she gets home, her attention deficit kicks in and she's off to the next Christmas cocktail party on her calendar. She forgets all about her worship experience and goes happily along her way. She has heart, but no depth.

Not Given to the Things of God

Jesus heads next to the home of a wealthy woman of high status in the community. She continues to live beyond her means both financially and physically, which constantly keeps her stretched to her limits. Jesus sits with her as she sits through Bible study. She's grateful she made time for it given all she has to do to get ready for all of her Christmas gatherings. She checks her watch, makes a few notes on her phone, and then hears the last part of the instructor's sentence: ". . . Jesus is our Prince of Peace. We need Him every moment of every hour." *So true*, she thinks to herself. Then it's time to go. Before she knows it, Christmastime has come and gone, months have passed, and she can't remember the last time she cracked open her Bible. From the outside looking in, people think she's got it all. But she's built her house and her life on sinking sand.

Guarded, Grounded, and Given Fully to God

Jesus has one more stop to make. He smiles as He makes His way up the walkway of a simple home surrounded by snow-covered pines. A woman opens the door and invites Him in. Together they sit by the light of the Christmas tree and talk about her children, her grandchildren, and her recent answers to prayer. Jesus marvels at her faith. She's overwhelmed by His love. Jesus leans in and gets serious for a moment. He encourages her to reach out to the neighbor who has seemed especially quiet these days. She needs some hope and encouragement. In fact, she's home today and could use a visit. Jesus also brings to mind a passage of Scripture that will come in handy in the days ahead. She's not sure what's up ahead, but she trusts Him and holds His words close to her heart.

Jesus speaks to us through His Word, through the inner nudges of the Holy Spirit, through others, and through everyday circumstances that the untrained ear might miss. God Himself tells His people, "This is My Son! Listen to Him!" How much more of a charge do we need?

Think about it. Those who cultivate a listening life and respond to what Jesus says—their lives will abound in fruit. They'll walk in power. And they'll continually enjoy fellowship with God. Scripture promises to the one who listens that they'll receive *even more revelation*. Whatever they know now is just a taste of the wisdom and insight to come. But for those who squander God's instruction, who dismiss His precious voice in their ear, even the little wisdom and insight they have will dissipate. So sad. What's more important than what God has to say?

There's nothing like God's presence. There's no substitute for His power. He's working in your life even now.

There's nothing like God's presence. There's no substitute for His power. He's working in your life even now. What if you were more present with God and with others this holiday season? What might God show you?

PREPARE HIM ROOM

King Jesus, I want to hear what You have to say. Open my ears that I may more clearly hear You. Open my eyes that I may see Your handiwork all around me. Forgive me for my constant one-sided approach to life. I go, I do, I speak, and then I fall exhausted into bed every day. I want to pause and be present in the moment, for that is where Your grace is. I want to listen—really listen—to what others have to say, and even more importantly, to what You have to say. Help me to live responsively to Your movement in my life. I want to grow in my capacity to hear from You, and I know that only comes with time and attention. So, I'm listening, Lord. What do You want to say to me?

Look Up

Fast today from the shallow busyness that drains the soul. Slow your pace and turn your face to the one whom this whole season is for. Put on some worship music; sit with your Bible and journal in your lap and listen. What is God saying to you? Write it down. Also, ask Him to show you who to pursue for the sole purpose of listening to them. You'll bless them greatly by your presence and your listening ear.

Day 9

A PHYSICAL AND SPIRITUAL KINGDOM

Today's Reading: Luke 9

OTHER PASSAGES TO PONDER

"Seek the Kingdom of God above all else, and live righteously, and he will give you everything you need." —Matthew 6:33

"Heal the sick, and tell them, 'The Kingdom of God is near you now.'" —Luke 10:9

Jesus announced his Kingdom by both PREACHING AND HEAL-
ING, *and he sent his disciples to do the same. If he had limited himself to preaching, people might have seen his Kingdom as spiritual
only. If he had healed without preaching, people might not have
realized the spiritual importance of his mission. . . . The truth about
Jesus is that he is both God and man, both spiritual and physical;
and the salvation that he offers is both for the soul and the body.*
—Life Application Study Bible [1]

Someone recently said, "We've got to get away from all
of this talk about soul care and get back to preaching
the gospel." Her statement, at first, sounds righteous and
biblical. And in many ways, she was right. Still, it made me
cringe. Not because we don't tend to focus too much on ourselves at the expense of the lost. Because we do. The reason
I didn't like her statement was because it felt sharp, lacked
compassion, and missed a crucial point.

It's true—Jesus came to seek and save the lost. But it's also
true that everywhere Jesus went, He tended to the human
soul. His compassion moved Him to heal the multitudes, to
deliver those tormented by demons, and to put right those
who were thinking wrong. Jesus loves us and cares deeply
about the human condition.

Even today, countless Christians sludge through life exhausted, burdened, and under-joyed. Does Jesus berate them

for the condition of their souls and tell them to get out there and do their job? No, He says,

> "Come to me, all of you who are weary and carry heavy burdens, and I will give you rest."
>
> Matthew 11:28

If you're overstressed this holiday season and it's entirely your fault, do know that Jesus cares. His invitation stands: *"Come to Me when you're weary."* You'll find Him with open arms and a tender heart. He won't shame you or rebuke you. He'll comfort you and give you rest. He'll teach you a better way to live. And He'll love you every step of the way.

If you're just plain weary from serving others at church, leaving you no time or energy to put into your family holiday, you can trust that God is not rolling His eyes at you or breathing a heavy sigh. He cares. He'll give you rest. Make room for Him. May the restorative power of Christ's kingdom come to your heart and your home this Christmas season.

Isaiah prophesied about the coming King. Let's look at a few verses from Isaiah chapter nine. Read these verses slowly and ponder the kind of King that God sent to earth; notice what He's like and what He cares about.

> Isaiah 9:2—The people who walk in darkness will see a great light. For those who live in a land of deep darkness, a light will shine.

Isaiah 9:4—For you will break the yoke of their slavery and lift the heavy burden from their shoulders.

Isaiah 9:6–7—For a child is born to us, a son is given to us. The government will rest on his shoulders. And he will be called: Wonderful Counselor, Mighty God, Everlasting Father, Prince of Peace. His government and its peace will never end. He will rule with fairness and justice from the throne of his ancestor David for all eternity. The passionate commitment of the LORD of Heaven's Armies will make this happen!

This is our God! Jesus doesn't save us to slave us. He saved us because He loves us. He has become our Prince of Peace. Our mighty Counselor. The everlasting God. And though He wants His kingdom to expand in and through us, He knows all about our tendencies and our trials. He knows how weak and self-focused we can be. So He teaches us, walks with us, and shows us how to grow.

After a long day of ministry, the disciples tried to slip away, but the crowds were relentless. Why? Because they desperately needed what Jesus offered. And He welcomed them with open arms. He told them about the kingdom—about His power not only to heal them but to save them.

The people desperately needed ministry. The disciples desperately needed rest. Jesus cared about them both. But this time He asked His disciples to stay engaged a little while longer. And so they did.

After what felt like a significant day of ministry, the disciples were once again ready to send the crowds away so the people could find something to eat and the disciples could get a much-needed break. Jesus responded, *"You feed them."* What? How? Read the story and ponder once again the significance of this miracle. Everyone ate to fullness, and there were baskets left over!

There's an African proverb that says, "A hungry stomach has no ears." In other words, if you don't tend to people's physical needs, they'll have no capacity to grasp their spiritual needs. Jesus cared deeply about the masses, about the demonic oppression, the chronic conditions, and the injuries that left people vulnerable and disabled. And He tended to those. But He was also *very* invested in training His disciples in the way of faith.

He ministered to those outside the faith with many miracles and His personal touch. He pointed them upward, to a new and everlasting kingdom.

And He trained those within the faith family by allowing them to encounter scenarios that were beyond them. He asked for their obedience and faith. He showed them how to operate in a kingdom power that exceeded their natural giftings or resources. Those who are willing to follow Jesus to such places of dependence will experience that same kingdom power today.

You know you're maturing in your faith when you begin to discern which aspect of the kingdom God is working on in you. Do you live in constant concern over your own needs, wants, and comfort even though Jesus has proven Himself to you time and time again? If so, perhaps it's time to seek God on a deeper level and discern the spiritual work He wants to do in you and around you. Maybe your problems aren't too big; maybe they're too small.[2] God wants you to believe Him and trust Him for greater things.

Maybe your problems aren't too big; maybe they're too small. God wants you to believe Him and trust Him for greater things.

Or maybe for you, it's been all about the spiritual aspect of this journey but you've neglected and de-prioritized your soul's needs—your mental, physical, and emotional health. If you've neglected your soul, you've likely done the same to those closest to you. Jesus doesn't overlook the soul. He *restores* our souls. Invite His presence and power to do a miracle work within you. He still does that, you know.

Maybe you're ready to finally step away and get some rest, but Jesus is asking for just a little more time and a lot more faith. Will you trust Him? This is not about your resources or even your bandwidth. God wants to train you in some of the higher ways of the kingdom. Trust that He'll do a great work through you and that He'll tend to your physical needs when the time is right.

Jesus' kingdom is an everlasting kingdom. It has come and is coming. He heals the sick, provides for the poor, gives rest to the weary and sight to the blind. He saves the lost, corrects the wanderer, forgives the sinner, and welcomes the prodigal. To seek first the kingdom of God this holiday season is to put Jesus at the very center of it all. It's to seek His will, His way, for His glory. And as you do, you'll be delighted to find that as you tend to that which is closest to God's heart—the lost, the hurting, the marginalized, the poor, and the outcast—He never stops caring for you.

PREPARE HIM ROOM

Mighty Savior, Everlasting God, Prince of Peace, Wonderful Counselor! Where do I begin? I want Your kingdom to come, Your will to be done, in me, through me, and all around me. I submit to Your rule and reign in my life. As I seek You first, You establish me in the way I should go. All of my priorities fall into place when I give You first place. Use me to tend the physical needs around me. And surprise me by doing a miraculous work in and through me. I declare this by faith: Everywhere I place my feet, Your kingdom comes to earth. Amen!

LOOK UP

Fast from overcommitment, soul neglect, and fretting over your limits. Accept the rest and grace Jesus offers you this very moment. View every aspect of your holiday season as an invitation to trust Jesus in a way you haven't before.

Day 10

MARVEL

Today's Reading: Luke 10

But to all who believed him and accepted him, he gave the right to become children of God. —John 1:12

But the person who is joined to the Lord is one spirit with him. —1 Corinthians 6:17

Receive this, the great miracle of mercy. Let the grace of God flow over you like a cleansing cascade, flushing out all dregs of guilt and shame. Nothing separates you from God. Your conscience may accuse you, but God accepts you. Others may dredge up your past, but God doesn't. As far as he is concerned, the work is once-and-for-all-time finished. —Max Lucado[1]

Sometime late in November or early December, I open my front door and hang our Christmas wreath on a gold hook. I step back, take it in, and we begin another Christmas holiday. It's weighty and beautiful. The circle of evergreen reminds me of Jesus' crown of thorns. The deep burgundy berries bring to mind the blood He spilled for humanity. The glistening gold bows speak of the unfathomable gift of eternal life He offers to all who call on His name and trust Him for salvation. My wreath symbolically speaks a message: *Blessings to all who enter here. As for me and my house, we will serve the Lord.*

I feel this conviction; I believe it with all my heart. I live for Jesus. Yet how often do I open the door of my heart at Christmastime to the very messages that speak a contrary word to what Jesus won for me?

Watch too many Christmas commercials in a row, and it won't be long until an uneasy sense of not-enough-ness settles in. Look too long at your old Christmas ornaments and decorations (some of which you bought last year), and you'll breathe a sigh under your breath that says, *Everything's old, nothing's new.* Attend a few well-done parties, and you'll feel convinced that you've got a long way to go to get your act together.

When you open the door to defeating and insecure thoughts, you take Christ right out of Christmas. Let's take each lie one by one. Watch all the perfect Christmas commercials if you'd like, but remind yourself that these are paid actors on a professional movie set with cameras, lights, and filters. All those people will go home to their messy lives at the end of the day. And that sense of not-enough-ness? When you follow Christ Jesus, your place in the Father's heart is so sturdy, so secure, you lack no good thing. Not a thing. Not-enough-ness doesn't belong in your vocabulary.

> All praise to God, the Father of our Lord Jesus Christ, who has blessed us with every spiritual blessing in the heavenly realms because we are united with Christ.
>
> Ephesians 1:3

How about your old decorations and ornaments? Purchasing a few fun ornaments is one thing. Allowing a lie to seep into your bones is another thing altogether. Picture your beautiful wreath on your front door. Embrace the symbolism of Jesus' victorious work on the cross. Now picture the enemy barging through your front door. He whisks right by your wreath, bumps it with his shoulder, and almost knocks it off its hook. He tracks in mud and spews accusations about all you lack in the way of home décor and ability. It may sound silly, but we've all lost joy over lesser things.

When Jesus walked out of that grave, He gave the word *new* a whole new meaning. He dismantled the enemy's case against us. He made a public spectacle of the devil when He stripped him of his power over us. Jesus ushered in a new day, a new kingdom, and offered a new beginning to anyone who would receive Him. He's *always* up to something new.

> And the one sitting on the throne said, "Look, I am making everything new!" And then he said to me, "Write this down, for what I tell you is trustworthy and true."
>
> Revelation 21:5

Finally, let's consider our tendency to compare and then despair. You go to a friend's party (that they've been preparing for all year) and you suddenly remember, *Um, I left a whole load of wet clothes in the washer.* You let your mind swirl with thoughts about your less-than-stellar performance as a human being. Once again, the enemy will use whatever means necessary to rob you of your joy and skew your perspective. These examples may seem like such small, trivial battles, but if they work on us, the enemy will waste his time on us.

> "The thief's purpose is to steal and kill and destroy. My purpose is to give them a rich and satisfying life."
>
> John 10:10

Have you noticed that the devil always goes after our worth, our position, and our performance? Why? Because Jesus won a sound victory against him on our behalf in all these areas. We possess all things in Christ. We're secure in Him. And we have nothing to prove. We must hang on to these unshakable truths no matter the season. Some of our Christmas holidays will feel almost magical; we'll remember them forever. Other times, we may endure such sorrow and hardship that we'll not forget those holidays for all the wrong reasons. And though we all want to enjoy a festive and fun holiday, we are (thankfully) anchored to Christ, not to a Christmas tree that could tip over at any moment.

In today's reading in the gospel of Luke, we watch as Jesus gathers together seventy disciples and sends them out, two by two. He empowers them to heal the sick, cast out demons, and declare that the kingdom of God is near. Once those same disciples saw firsthand the power available to them in Christ Jesus, they came running back and proclaimed, "Lord, even the demons obey us!"

> *Though we all want to enjoy a festive and fun holiday, we are (thankfully) anchored to Christ, not to a Christmas tree that could tip over at any moment.*

Jesus essentially replies, *"Do not marvel that the demons obey you. I've given you authority over them. Marvel that your name is written in the Book of Life. You've been taken out of the kingdom of darkness and transferred into My kingdom! Yes, I have given you the great gift of authority. But even more importantly, I've given you My identity. Use My authority to defeat the enemy. But walk in My identity because I won it for you. No one can snatch you out of My hand. It's not what you do that establishes you. It's who you are in Me that holds you fast. Never forget that you're not the sum of your past mistakes or even the accumulation of all your achievements. If you make the mistake of tying your identity to your performance, you set yourself up to be deceived. If the wonder of what I empower you to do upstages what I accomplish on that Cross, you've already lost your way. Keep yourself anchored to Me. I am your strong tower—your secure place. You possess all because you are in Me, and I am in you."*

Prepare Him Room

Lord, all too often I get impressed with the wrong things. I marvel at someone's ability to decorate a home but never stop to think about what You accomplished for me. It's truly a miracle, Lord. I'm brand-new, through and through. I'm a part of a royal family line. I've been grafted in because of what You did on the Cross for me. I marvel that You saved me. I marvel that I have constant and continual access to You. I marvel that You offer me new mercies and a new sunrise every single morning. How blessed am I? Grow a thankful heart within me, oh Lord. You deserve it. I love You. Amen.

Look Up

Fast from boredom, complaining, comparing, and self-criticizing. Look up and look around and find countless reasons for giving thanks. Above all, marvel over the miracle of your salvation.

Day 11

ASK, DON'T DEMAND

Today's Reading: Luke 11

True humility and fear of the LORD
    lead to riches, honor, and long life. —Proverbs 22:4

And even when you ask, you don't get it because your motives
are all wrong—you want only what will give you pleasure.
—James 4:3

*God is not a genie in a bottle, and your wish is not His command.
His command better be your wish. . . . Until His sovereign will
becomes your sanctified wish, your prayer life will be unplugged
from its power supply. —Mark Batterson* [1]

J esus had an active prayer life. Imagine what it was like for the disciples to watch Jesus slip away to get alone with the Father. They no doubt also witnessed moments of impromptu prayer when Jesus got quiet, looked up, and whispered a prayer for guidance. They walked with Him day in and day out and saw firsthand what an intimate, thriving walk with Almighty God looks like.

Imagine Jesus, in a secluded place, on His knees, hands open, eyes upward. Picture His countenance as the Father imparts wisdom, direction, and affection. The corners of Jesus' lips turn upward as He returns the praise back to His Abba. Just then, He hears sandals shuffling in the dirt and finds one of His disciples approaching Him slowly, watching Him intently. The disciple steps closer and says, "Lord, teach me, teach *us*, how to pray as You pray." Together they walk back toward the others, and Jesus unveils the Lord's Prayer.

Our Father, holy, holy is Your name. Your kingdom come, Your will be done. . . . Jesus taught them how to give God all the honor and glory He deserves, how to stay present in the moment with their ever-present Father and trust Him for all they would ever need, how to forgive as they'd been forgiven. Then, Jesus took the lesson of prayer to unchartered territory for the disciples. He told the story about a man who, late at night, asked a friend for some bread because of an unexpected houseguest. The man refused to be inconvenienced at such a late hour. Here's what Jesus said:

"But I tell you this—though he won't do it for friendship's sake, if you keep knocking long enough, he will get up and give you whatever you need because of your shameless persistence. And so I tell you, keep on asking, and you will receive what you ask for. Keep on seeking, and you will find. Keep on knocking, and the door will be opened to you. For everyone who asks, receives. Everyone who seeks, finds. And to everyone who knocks, the door will be opened."

Luke 11:8–10

Phillips Brooks, the great nineteenth-century preacher, said, "Prayer is not conquering God's reluctance, but taking hold upon God's willingness."[2] Jesus had an active prayer life. He wants us to have an active prayer life. Scripture tells us time and time again: Don't hold back! Pray! Don't worry about *anything*. Pray about *everything*. Tell God what you need, and don't forget to thank Him for what He's done. If you do this, you will experience a peace that will flood your soul and guard your heart and mind as you trust in Him.[3]

So go ahead, ask for provision. Seek His wisdom. Knock on the doors of heaven. They're bursting with divine supply. God wants you to want His influence.

But interestingly, note that Jesus invites us to ask for what we need, and then He promises to give us more of the Holy Spirit. What? When we have physical needs, don't they require physical answers? Well, yes. And God is so good to answer our physical needs with physical answers. But He wants us to value a deeper treasure that we've inherited because we are in Him.

When God gives us more of the Holy Spirit to meet our need, it may look something like this: You ask for money to pay your bills, and not only does the Holy Spirit nudge someone to send you a gift, He gives you wisdom about next steps you might need to take. You ask God to loosen up your schedule so that you won't feel so stressed, and the Holy Spirit drops divine wisdom into your heart about necessary adjustments and future commitments. You ask God to change a difficult family member, preferably before your Christmas gathering, and instead, He changes you. He offers you a fresh perspective on places within you that still need healing. He helps you not to take things personally. Then He offers insight into the brokenness in your family member, and He stirs up compassion in you. What a gift!

> *So go ahead, ask for provision. Seek His wisdom. Knock on the doors of heaven. They're bursting with divine supply.*

A little later, in Luke 11, Jesus warns against unbelief. People pressed, *asked* for a sign to prove that He is who He says He is. Earlier He invited His disciples to ask and keep asking, to seek and keep seeking. Yet here in this moment, Jesus didn't appreciate that people *asked* for a sign. The fact that Jesus invites His followers to ask and keep asking but then confronts bystanders for asking begs us to scoot in a little closer and seek to understand.

Let's go back to the disciple who watched Jesus pray. Picture him there with open hands and wide-eyed wonder when suddenly a host of questions spills from his lips. "Lord, teach me to pray like that. That calmness in your eyes—do you never feel fear? How come when you pray for healing, it happens every time, but not for us? What are we missing?"

Now picture a suspicious, hard-hearted, legalistic by-stander among the crowd of curious hearts. He spews, "I'll believe it when I see it. Prove that You are who You say you are, and I'll get back to You on my decision. I'm not easily fooled."

Though Jesus deeply loves the hard-hearted legalist (He saved and radically transformed Paul), He distances Him-self from the proud and draws near and gives grace to the humble.[4] Asking for wisdom and demanding a sign are two very different things.

We are all a pile of contradictions, especially at Christ-mastime. We're grateful, and then we're grumpy. We're glad, and then we're mad. One minute we're all about the festivi-ties, and the next moment we're counting the days until it's all over. When you watch those Christmas movies portraying a rich, spoiled, demanding child next to a poor, grateful, re-ceptive child, who do you root for? Perhaps this is why Jesus said, "*Blessed* are the poor in spirit, for theirs is the kingdom of heaven."[5] So what can we learn from Jesus' insights on the difference between asking and demanding?

Jesus asks you to trust Him and believe what He says about Himself. Everything about our Christian life flows from the reality of who He truly is. Everything about our faith is built on this foundational precept:

> In the beginning the Word already existed.
>   The Word was with God,
>   and the Word was God.
> He existed in the beginning with God.
> God created everything through him,
>   and nothing was created except through him.
> The Word gave life to everything that was created,
>   and his life brought light to everyone.
> The light shines in the darkness,
>   and the darkness can never extinguish it.
>
> John 1:1–5

The more we trust that Jesus *is* who He says He is, the more we change from the inside out. We behave like children—and not in a good way—when we never mature out of an insistence that God prove Himself time and time again by giving us what we want when we want it. He owes us nothing. Has nothing to prove. He gave us everything. His life for ours. It's unfathomable.

Yet, Jesus invites us to approach Him—with wide-eyed wonder—and ask that all of who He is would come in and change all of who we are. Christmas is all in the heart. The gospel is all in the heart. How we see Jesus in the depths of our hearts impacts how boldly we approach Him and how audaciously we dare to ask Him to do the impossible in our midst. We're on solid, biblical ground to pray such bold prayers. Jesus said, *"When your eye is good, your whole body is filled with light."*[6]

Prepare Him Room

Lord Jesus, I want everything You have for me. I repent of and reject any notion that I'm entitled to something I don't have at the moment. You give good gifts to Your children. You withhold no good thing from us. If I don't have it yet, it's because it's not good for me yet. I trust You, Lord. I bow before You and honor You as my King. I open my hands and ask You to fill them. Whatever You want to entrust to me, Lord, I'll take it. Lead me on, gentle Savior. I'm Yours. Amen.

Look Up

Fast from entitlement of any kind. Be patient with the checkout clerk. Leave a large tip, regardless of the service. Entrust your not-yets to God and enjoy the life you have now.

PRIDE AND PRESENTATION

Today's Reading: Luke 12

OTHER PASSAGES TO PONDER

But don't be afraid of those who threaten you. For the time is coming when everything that is covered will be revealed, and all that is secret will be made known to all. —Matthew 10:26

> Fearing people is a dangerous trap,
> but trusting the Lord means safety.
> —Proverbs 29:25

I want to look beyond my preferences and admirations, my insecurities and assumptions, my appraisals and fears. I want to stop asking,

"How does this person see me?" and instead understand, "How can I really see them?" —Holley Gerth[1]

Years ago, we attended a Christmas party that left me feeling discouraged, frustrated, and judgmental. The pomp and circumstance nauseated me because I happened to know that the employees who worked for this couple struggled beneath a heavy load and made minimal wages while the couple lived with opulence and privilege. I didn't want to be there.

I love Christmastime, and for the life of me, nothing about this gathering felt festive or Christlike. They impressed and intimidated most everyone at the party. I, in turn, judged them. Not the right reaction, I know. I don't blame them. My bad attitude came from within me. But it's interesting how the seeds of pride never bear good fruit.

In today's Scripture reading, the crowds elbowed and shoved their way to get a good look at Jesus and hear what He had to say. Jesus' eyes scanned the multitudes, and then He focused on His disciples and said:

> "Beware of the yeast of the Pharisees—their hypocrisy. The time is coming when everything that is covered up will be revealed, and all that is secret will be made known to all."

Luke 12:1–2

Pharisees prided themselves on being large and in charge. They were the ones who established the standard and judged those who fell short. They presented themselves one way but lived another. They appeared to be holy, but they were corrupt to their core. Maybe they started out with hearts for God, but in due time, they fell in love with the power, the leverage, and the accolades that accompanied their role. They loved their rules but not the people entrusted to their care.

It's easy to stand at a distance and roll our eyes over such arrogance. But Jesus warned His disciples and He warns us for a reason: Left to our own devices, many of us are inexplicably drawn to being in control or in an important role. Nothing wrong with that when you're a natural-born leader. But there's everything wrong with it when you want the position for how it serves you and not so you can serve others.

How many ministry leaders—if they're honest—crave the attention they receive when they walk into a room or an event? But it's not just ministry leaders. How many moms love to be the center of neighborhood conversations? How many corporate climbers vie for position because they want to be the one calling the shots?

It's impossible to love others when your goal is to impress them. We're not capable of serving others when we have an insatiable appetite to be served, lauded, and hailed.

Jesus first warned the disciples about the leaven of pride and hypocrisy. Then He took it a step further and told them:

"Whatever *you* have said in the dark will be heard in the light, and what *you* have whispered behind closed doors will be shouted from the housetops for all to hear!"

Luke 12:3 (emphasis mine)

Jesus cautioned them, basically saying, *"If you allow this leaven to infect your soul, if you become someone who says one thing and does another, if you grow to love man's praise more than you do My glory, if you start to care more about your image than you do the lowly and the hurting in your midst, well, in due time your hypocrisy will come to light. Beware of the leaven! Even the smallest bit can ruin your soul."*

Let that sink in for a moment. God is so opposed to pride that He'll expose it wherever He finds it, even when it's in the heart of a believer. This puts the fear of God in me. When pride seeps into our soul, it pushes out fruit that will always honor us and dishonor God. When we develop an appetite for power, position, or presentation, we will justify or spiritualize many things to hang on to our idol. It's sobering to fathom that if there's any private scheming to put ourselves above others, it will one day come to light.

In this instance, Jesus charges His disciples to beware of and guard against such influence. In other words, Jesus is saying, *"Follow My example. Love people. Hope in God. Your name is written in the Book of Life. Man's praise and admiration are dust compared to such a glory. Don't get infected with the worldly lust for power that grows in the dark. It'll destroy you. It'll also expose you. One day it'll be brought into the light."*

In another instance, Jesus spoke of darkness and light but from a different angle. In Matthew's gospel, Jesus prepared His disciples for persecution. Read what He said to His followers and notice how He uses some of the same words to convey a completely different message:

> "But don't be afraid of those who threaten you. For the time is coming when everything that is covered will be revealed, and all that is secret will be made known to all. *What I tell you now in the darkness, shout abroad when daybreak comes. What I whisper in your ear, shout from the housetops for all to hear!"*
>
> Matthew 10:26–27 (emphasis mine)

In this instance, Jesus charges His disciples: *"All I've taught you in the shadows—step into the light and proclaim it for the world to hear! What I whisper in your ear—steward it, apply it to your life, teach it to others. Don't shrink back in the face of prideful, posturing leaders. Do not fear them. Leaven grows in the dark and will one day be brought into the light for all to see. The words you've heard me teach in the dark will one day be broadcast for the world to hear. All tribes, nations, and tongues will know that I am God! Don't wait until that time to live brave and bold."*

How much precious energy do we waste trying to impress others? How often do we give precious mental space to what others might think of us? How often are we intimidated by people in positions of power?

Luke chapter twelve follows an interesting progression. First, Jesus cautions against the leaven of the Pharisees. *"Guard against every kind of greed,"* Jesus said. Then He addressed worry and its damaging impact to the soul. Don't strive for position. Don't worry about possessions. Then He brings it home: *"Live ready for My return."*

You want to see splendor and fanfare? When the skies open up and the King of Glory returns, the whole world will know it. Every knee will bow and every tongue will confess that Jesus is and always has been who He says He is.

Don't strive for position. Don't worry about possessions. Live ready for Christ's return.

Try to picture every person on the earth and those who've passed from this life to the next, all on their knees, trembling in awe. Now imagine that same King, our smiling Savior. He ushers you into a royal banquet where He spared no expense. Picture opulent table settings and candelabras, music, food, and fellowship galore; celebration, tears of joy, and stories all around. There'll be no prideful posturing or pretense. Just holy awe and wonder that by God's grace, we are heirs of God; we have a seat at the table of grace.

For those He finds full of faith, about His business, living expectantly for Him, Jesus promises that when He returns,

He will put on an apron, pull out a chair, and serve *us* as His guests of honor.

Prepare Him Room

King Jesus, show me my heart. Keep me close to You. I refuse to be intimidated by those who idolize their position and who misuse their power. Help me to stay confident with a humble, pure heart. I trust You to make things right when the time is right. Help me to confidently shine a light on all You've taught me. I want to walk that narrow path of holy confidence and humble dependence. I will follow You, Lord. Amen.

Look Up

Fast from intimidation. Guard your heart against cynicism. Refuse inferiority and insecurity. Embrace holy confidence.

Day 13

CONTEND FOR THE FAITH

Today's Reading: Luke 13

Therefore, since we are surrounded by such a huge crowd of witnesses to the life of faith, let us strip off every weight that slows us down, especially the sin that so easily trips us up. And let us run with endurance the race God has set before us. —Hebrews 12:1

Fight the good fight for the true faith. Hold tightly to the eternal life to which God has called you, which you have declared so well before many witnesses. —1 Timothy 6:12

Paul uses active and forceful verbs to describe the Christian life; run, pursue, fight, hold tightly. Some think Christianity is a passive religion that advocates waiting for God to act. On the contrary, we must have an active faith, training, working hard, sacrificing, and doing what we know is right. —Life Application Study Bible[1]

We work hard at many things. We work hard to make a life for ourselves, to appear a certain way to others, to lose weight, to pay our bills, and to keep the peace. Sometimes we even work hard to avoid conflict, to stay comfortable and un-challenged, and as a result, we never change or grow.

Our souls find rest when we stop all our striving and more deeply *know* that He is God (see Psalm 46:10). But there are some things that are worth our effort. It's good to work hard to contend for the faith, to forgive others, and to love well. It's wise to want to be people of our word, to do excellent work, to fight for our marriages, to be debt free, and to make family a priority.

It's a colossal waste of our time to put all kinds of energy into managing others' opinions of us. We actually damage ourselves when we prioritize comfort and ease to the point that we become soft and useless in the great battle between good and evil.

Though it's sometimes difficult to follow Jesus, is it also difficult to be saved? Why did Jesus say these words?

"Work hard to enter the narrow door to God's Kingdom, for many will try to enter but will fail."

Luke 13:24

The NIV translation reads: "Make every effort to enter through the narrow door." The phrase "work hard," or "make every effort," translates this way: *to enter a contest; to contend with adversaries; to struggle with difficulties and dangers; to endeavor with strenuous zeal; to strive to obtain something.*[2]

Doesn't that just describe this faith journey? *To enter a contest; to contend with adversaries; to struggle with difficulties; to strive to obtain something.* We battle a very real enemy who looks for every opportunity to steal what belongs to us. We fall down and we get back up again. We feel battered and bruised one day and blessed and bold the next. We run this race to win the prize. We engage with God and His promises to lay hold of everything Christ won for us.

If you've followed Jesus closely for any length of time, you know it's a hard road sometimes. But what *did* Jesus mean when He urged those who've not yet trusted Him to *work hard to enter the narrow door*? Perhaps a look at the Amplified translation will shed some light for us:

"Strive to enter through the narrow door [force aside unbelief and the attractions of sin]; for many, I tell you, will try to enter [by their own works] and will not be able."

Luke 13:24 AMP

Some have interpreted this verse to mean that we need to earn our salvation, yet Scripture clearly promises that salvation is a free gift, acquired by grace through faith (see Ephesians 2:8–9).

Picture with me the crowds that pressed in to listen to Jesus. Some wanted to learn from Him, others wanted to trap Him. Some were mildly interested in what He had to say, while others hung on His every word.

Now consider the Christmas holiday. Don't you find very much the same slice of life? Some embrace this season because they nobly desire to gather with family and friends and remember that our truest gifts are the people that surround us. They may not feel the urgency to know Jesus personally, but they view the holiday as a good opportunity to gather. And that's true; it is. But there's much, much more to this season than simply having a good time. Others are so jaded by the commercialism (understandably so) that they count the days until it's all over. Sadly, some approach this season with a shoulder shrug of indifference. Still, others are absolutely captivated afresh that Jesus came to earth for *them*.

If you could peel back the sky and see into the spiritual realm, you'd see a cosmic spiritual battle between light and darkness, between God's warring angels and Satan's scheming demons. All the while, lost people go through life on earth totally unaware of the value of their souls and of an eternity that hangs in the balance.

When someone takes a step toward Jesus in any way, enemy opposition will always be close at hand. For some to take Jesus seriously, they have to overcome hurdles of unbelief, fear of man, and the attraction of sin just to get to a place where they're willing to humbly admit their need for a savior. And you can know that in such cases, the enemy won't just step aside and pave a way for a person to leave his kingdom of darkness and to join God's army of redeemed saints.

If you could peel back the sky and see into the spiritual realm, you'd see a cosmic spiritual battle between light and darkness, between God's warring angels and Satan's scheming demons.

Consider Muslims who decide to follow Christ. They have much to overcome to follow Jesus. Almost always it costs them their family, their friendships, their home, and even their sense of honor among their people. Sometimes it costs them their very lives. We in the West cannot relate to paying such a price for following Jesus. Unfortunately, since that's so, we can also settle into a false sense of security about our eternity. We may think that since we belong to a great church, and we love the music, and we have a few Christian friends, we're good. Association is not the same as transformation.

In this thirteenth chapter of Luke's gospel, we see Jesus urging people *not* to embrace a false sense of security.

How was it that some people ate and drank with Jesus and listened to His preaching only to have Jesus say, "Go away. I never knew you!"? Hear what they're saying? "We ate with you, drank with you, and listened to you." A jarring revelation, no? Consumer religion doesn't save us.

Jesus made it clear then, and we still miss it today. Though salvation is a free gift, we lay hold of it by entering through a narrow way. We let go of the idea that we can save ourselves. We've no laurels on which to stand, no earthly associations that guarantee our entrance. We come humbly to Jesus, we acknowledge and repent of our sin, we confess that He, indeed, is the Savior of the world, and we receive a priceless treasure in return: the unfathomable gift of salvation.

Though it's simple to be saved, none of this comes easy. Jesus paid a brutal price for our freedom. We have to get over ourselves and admit we need saving if we want to enjoy the free gift of salvation, if we want the Spirit of the living God to take up residence in our souls, and if we want to know for certain that our eternity is secure in Christ Jesus. And even though our eternity is secure, Jesus promised we'd experience trouble and hardship. But He also promised that we would overcome. We follow a conquering Savior who's deeply committed to getting us safely home.

> Now all glory to God, who is able to keep you from fall-
> ing away and will bring you with great joy into his glorious
> presence without a single fault. All glory to him who alone

is God, our Savior through Jesus Christ our Lord. All glory, majesty, power, and authority are his before all time, and in the present, and beyond all time! Amen.

Jude 1:24–25

Prepare Him Room

King Jesus, I owe everything to You. How can I ever thank You enough for Your gift to me? You came to earth, lived a vulnerable life, and died a brutal death for me. You shattered the enemy's claim on my life and brought me into the family! Help me to run my race with eternity in mind. Help me to fight the good fight and to help others get free as well. May the power of Your Spirit overwhelm us all this holiday season. Amen.

Look Up

Consider your strivings, rest secure in Christ, and fast from any obsession with appearances, opinions, and un-appointed (not God-given) obligations. Also, do a few hard things this season: tell the enemy to shut his mouth; put fear under your feet; admit to someone that you follow Jesus; forgive that one family member.

Prayer of Salvation:

Dear Jesus, I confess that I am a sinner and I need saving. I cannot save myself. I cannot perform well enough to secure my eternity or to earn my way into the royal family. Only grace can do that for me. I believe that You lived a sinless life, that You died on the Cross for my sins, and that You rose again on the third day. You defeated sin and death on my behalf! You did this for me! Please, come into my life, forgive me of my sin; cleanse me from all unrighteousness, and make me new again. Fill me with Your Holy Spirit and change me from the inside out. Today I turn away from my old life of sin and striving that I may follow You. I believe with my heart and confess with my mouth that You are my Lord and that my eternity is secure because of You. Thank you for this indescribable gift, dear Jesus! One day I will see You face-to-face. I'm forever grateful. Amen.

Day 14

SEE THE STORY

Today's Reading: Luke 14

OTHER PASSAGES TO PONDER

"Be still and know (recognize, understand) that I am God.
I will be exalted among the nations! I will be exalted in the
   earth." —Psalm 46:10 AMP

Trust in and rely confidently on the LORD with all your heart
And do not rely on your own insight or understanding.
In all your ways know and acknowledge and recognize Him,
   And He will make your paths straight and smooth
      [removing obstacles that block your way].
      —Proverbs 3:5–6 AMP

I wonder—how many situations that we would call "disappoint-ments," "hassles" and "setbacks" might actually be the loving hand of God trying to slow us down for the sake of our souls, and so that we might receive him? —*John Eldredge*[1]

I'd waited years for my perfect Christmas holiday. I thought there was such a thing. It's terrifically cliché, I know. I peeked into the living room, where my husband worked to assemble our new and sizeable Christmas tree (handed down from Kev's parents), only to find him perplexed and unsettled. Apparently, during his spring cleaning the previous year, he accidentally disposed of half of our good tree and most of our Charlie Brown poor excuse for a tree, leaving him with less than two halves of two very different trees.

At least last year I had a tree.

Kev pulled out his tools and extension cords and went to work. The living room looked like a construction zone. I didn't get to have my family Christmas decorating day like I'd hoped. I kissed the top of my hardworking husband's head, put the kids to bed, and went to bed myself. I awoke a few hours later to find the other side of the bed empty. I went out into the living room and found my dear husband seated on the floor. He held the Christmas light remote like it was a Christmas miracle and stared up at the best Christmas tree we'd ever had.

I crawled into his lap and marveled at what had transpired in just a few short hours. This was our tree. Through the mess and the mishap emerged a gift I'd not soon forget. So much had gone wrong in our lives. Sickness, medical debt, and one deferred hope after another. Yet through it all, God was up to something good, building something beautiful in our lives, something I could not see through the mess.

I wanted relief. God was after the total redemption of our story.

We don't often like God's ways. He seems content to be misunderstood. He's willing to take us on a journey that makes no sense to us. For instance, when it came time for Jesus' grand entrance into the world, why was it through the womb of a teenage girl? Why was He born into poverty? Why would He create a virgin birth knowing many would consider this story scandalous and find it more offensive than inviting? Why was there no room in the inn for the Savior of the world? Surely this wasn't a detail that escaped His notice.

I wanted relief. God was after the total redemption of our story.

God's chosen people were painfully oppressed by the Romans, and they longed for and looked for the prophesied King who would finally deliver them and acknowledge them as God's chosen people. Yet it would be years before they understood that Jesus came to set their very souls free, not just their nation.

Why does it seem that God so often does things the hard way?

Have you noticed that He sometimes answers our prayers one slow, small detail at a time? He helps us to gain ground, but more often than not, only by inches at a time. But given the fact that He's infinitely loving and wise and He's a really good Father who gives good gifts to His children, there *must* be a reason He allows such trials, mysteries, and delays to coexist with His goodness.

The King of the universe, the one who spoke the galaxies into existence, is actually after something much deeper in us than our finite minds can conceive. And He's always up to something we cannot fully discern, something we may not see the value of now. But we will later. Our God came to earth through the womb of a teenage girl to show the world His heart for the least and the low-liest by the world's standards. He knew full well what He was doing, though it may take us our lifetime to fully comprehend it.

God is in the process of conform-ing us to the image of His dear Son. He's teaching us to grow comfort-able with mystery. There *will* be some things we just can't explain,

> *God is in the process of conforming us to the image of His dear Son. He's teaching us to grow comfortable with mystery.*

formulas that don't work, outcomes that make no sense *in the moment*. And He asks us to trust Him, to be tethered to

His goodness no matter how much our temporary seasons shake us.

Our process of transformation comes not from the path of ease, but from uphill climbs, raging storms, and enemy opposition. It comes from engaging our faith when our circumstances speak a contrary message. It comes from continual interaction with our Father, just as Jesus modeled for us. God guides and provides, corrects and directs; He humbles us, and He helps us. We need Him every hour.

> "My thoughts are nothing like your thoughts," says the
>   LORD.
>   "And my ways are far beyond anything you could
>   imagine.
> For just as the heavens are higher than the earth,
>   so my ways are higher than your ways
>   and my thoughts higher than your thoughts."
>
> Isaiah 55:8–9

The Pharisees invited Jesus to dinner in hopes of trapping Him into saying something that would condemn Him. Jesus offered more than words. He healed a man before their very eyes. On the Sabbath. *Think higher, see deeper.*

People postured for the honorable positions at the table. Jesus cautioned them against thinking more highly of themselves than they ought. Better to be humble and let God promote you than to self-promote and be humbled by God. While they postured to honor themselves, Jesus told them to honor those the world discards. *Think higher, see deeper.* He spoke of the inconvenient cost of following Him. Family members may not like it. People may judge you the way they judged Him. *Think higher, see deeper.* When you set out to be a serious follower of Christ, you'll find a thousand excuses to tend to temporary things like they're the most important things in the world. But eternal rewards come from eternal priorities. *Think higher, see deeper.*

Over and over again, Jesus urged people to open their eyes and see the coming kingdom. See the story God is writing on the earth through His Son!

You may be walking through a difficult season right now. Lift your gaze. God is up to something good and you can trust Him. One day, your eyes will see it. You may be so busy with the temporary that you've lost sight of the eternal. Today is a good day to push pause, step back, and think eternity. Your current season is packed with eternal possibilities. You may be on the receiving end of ridicule because of your sincere faith. You are not alone. Rejoice. Great is your reward in heaven.[2] *Think higher, see deeper.*

Prepare Him Room

Jesus, help me to see what You're up to in my midst. I don't want to be so bent on getting my way that I miss Your way. What do You want to say to me here? Give me eyes to see, ears to hear, and a heart to do Your will. I know You're writing an incredible story on the earth today. I want to step into my part and live it with holy conviction and passion. You're making something wonderful out of me, and I embrace the process. I trust You, Lord. Amen.

Look Up

Fast from making premature assessments about your story. If your story is not good yet, it's because God is not done yet.[3] Step back from your circumstances and ask God for a fresh revelation of who He is and how He is. Ask God to show you if your priorities are out of order. Rest in the reality that God's ways are higher than your ways and His ways are good.

JESUS PURSUES THE WANDERER

Today's Reading: Luke 15

OTHER PASSAGES TO PONDER

"For this is what the Sovereign LORD says: I myself will search for my sheep and look after them." —Ezekiel 34:11 NIV

All of us must die eventually. Our lives are like water spilled out on the ground, which cannot be gathered up again. But God does not just sweep life away; instead, he devises ways to bring us back when we have been separated from him. —2 Samuel 14:14

"In our world too, a stable once had something inside it that was bigger than our whole world." —C. S. Lewis[1]

For many believers, Christmastime stirs up both angst and anticipation. On one hand, we love preparing for our holiday gatherings, imagining our families together once again. And yet, on the other hand, those gatherings can be painful reminders of how lost some of our loved ones are. We get a closeup look at their lives. We hear unbiblical perspectives spill out of their mouths, and our hearts quietly sink in despair. We keep smiling. Keep serving. But secretly we wonder if God will ever open their eyes and capture their hearts.

That's why Luke chapter fifteen is such a gift to us this season. Jesus came to seek and save the lost. And you know what? He continues to seek and save the lost! Right now, He's pursuing your lost loved ones with a loving clarity and compassion that far outweighs your own. In this chapter, Jesus uses three different scenarios to convey His passionate heart for those who've lost their way. Let's look at the story.

Right now, Jesus is pursuing your lost loved ones with a loving clarity and compassion that far outweighs your own.

One day the Pharisees complained that Jesus ate with "filthy" people like tax collectors and known sinners—

people who purposely did things they knew they shouldn't. Jesus even had the audacity to share a meal with them! I love that Jesus didn't suddenly become self-conscious, like He was caught in the act of wandering Himself. No, Jesus knew who He was, where He was, and what He was doing there. With tender strength, Jesus looked at the Pharisees and painted three descriptive word pictures for them. He first told the story about a shepherd who owned a hundred sheep. One of the sheep wandered off and got lost. What did the shepherd do? He left the ninety-nine and journeyed high and low to find the one. When the shepherd found the lost sheep stuck in the thicket, he ran to the sheep, helped him get unstuck, and then put the frightened sheep over his shoulders and *joyfully* carried him back to the fold.

> "And when he has found it, he will joyfully carry it home on his shoulders."
>
> Luke 15:5

Next, Jesus offered the Pharisees a different analogy to further illustrate His priorities and passion.

> "Or suppose a woman has ten silver coins and loses one. Won't she light a lamp and sweep the entire house and search carefully until she finds it? And when she finds it, she will call in her friends and neighbors and say, 'Rejoice with me because I have found my lost coin.'"
>
> Luke 15:8–9

Palestinian women often received silver coins as a wedding gift, which made the coins especially valuable to her.[2]

I love that Jesus used this analogy! A woman with a wedding gift. Her prized possession. These coins represented her wedding, her marriage, and gifts from loved ones. The coins weren't just valuable in the practical sense; they represented union, celebration, and love. We are the bride of Christ. We were the *joy* set before Jesus that helped Him endure the cross and defeat its shame. Imagine that. Jesus all bloodied and battered, heaving that heavy cross down a rough road to the taunts and jeers of clueless onlookers. Yet, He still had joy in His heart. He had *you* in His heart. He had your lost loved one in His heart. And, in the midst of the worst circumstances imaginable, it brought Him great joy to persevere for the sake of those who would one day turn to Him. Unfathomable, no?

Before we move to Jesus' third illustration, it's important to note that the first two analogies only go so far. They reveal God's passion for the one who has lost his or her way. But here's where the analogies break down. The shepherd didn't know where the sheep had gone. The woman had no idea how or where her coin had been misplaced. When we or our loved ones are lost, it's not to say that Jesus doesn't know where we went. We may have lost our way, but Jesus always knows where we are. We can never escape His notice. He knows everything about us—when we stand up and when we sit down. He even knows what we're going to say before we say it.

O LORD, you have examined my heart and know
　　everything about me.
You know when I sit down or stand up. You know my
　　thoughts even when I'm far away.
You see me when I travel and when I rest at home.
　　You know everything I do. You know what I am
　　going to say
　　even before I say it, LORD. You go before me and
　　follow me.
　　You place your hand of blessing on my head. Such
　　knowledge is too wonderful for me, too great for
　　me to understand!

Psalm 139:1–6

Jesus used these illustrations to show that the wandering heart is never far from His heart. He seeks the lost because they don't know they're lost. It's the sick that need a doctor, not those who are convinced they are well. In pursuit of those He loves, Jesus orchestrates situations that bring truth and revelation to their hearts. He puts the right person in the right place at the right time. His Holy Spirit whispers truth at a moment of vulnerability. His warring angels intervene on enemy schemes to give the person a chance to repent.

As a radio host, I've heard countless stories from Christian leaders who've shared about their wandering ways. One man was at a party with a drink in his hand when he heard the whisper, "Is this really how you want to live? I have better plans for you." He put down his drink, walked away from the party lifestyle, and came running back to God.

Which brings us to Jesus' third illustration for the Pharisees: the prodigal son story. In the first two illustrations, the owner searches fervently for the lost. In this illustration, the father waits expectantly for his return. Both ideas represent the Father's heart. He's both pursuing those who wander and waiting expectantly for their return. He doesn't force His way on us. He works and He waits while we go along our way.

In all three scenarios, Jesus makes a point to describe the party in heaven when one lost soul repents and turns to Jesus. Picture confetti, cheers, celebration, and feasts. All for the one. Every heart matters to Jesus. That's why He came, why He lived, why He endured a torturous death, and why He blew the doors off the grave—to make a way for us to spend forever with Him in eternity. What if we pursued the lost as fervently, waited as expectantly, and celebrated as wildly as the angels in heaven?

Be of good cheer this season. Jesus is on a rescue mission. He will search out the nooks and crannies of this world to shepherd His children back to His heart.

PREPARE HIM ROOM

Precious Jesus, thank You for how You relentlessly pursue the wandering heart. You carry the world on Your shoulders and my loved ones in Your heart. I can't save them, but You can. Draw them by the power of Your Spirit back to You, back to us. Move miraculously in their lives that they may know that there's a God in heaven who knows their name and loves them deeply. In the meantime, I'll celebrate the gifts in front of me. So much for which to be grateful. I'll start there. Thank You, Lord. Amen.

LOOK UP

Fast from angst, worry, and despair over your lost loved ones. Release them to God and trust Him to work in ways you cannot imagine. Celebrate the small victories you see. Don't minimize, don't "Yeah, but," and don't miss the fact that God is moving even now. Ask Him to open your eyes to see it.

Day 16

SHREWD, NOT SCROOGE

Today's Reading: Luke 16

OTHER PASSAGES TO PONDER

You groped your way through that murk once, but no longer. You're out in the open now. The bright light of Christ makes your way plain. So no more stumbling around. Get on with it! The good, the right, the true—these are the actions appropriate for daylight hours. Figure out what will please Christ, and then do it. —Ephesians 5:8–10 MSG

But friends, you're not in the dark, so how could you be taken off guard by any of this? You're sons of Light, daughters of Day. We live under wide open skies and know where we stand. So let's not sleepwalk through life like those others. Let's keep our eyes open and be smart. People sleep at night and get drunk at night. But not us! Since we're creatures of Day, let's act like it. Walk out into the daylight sober, dressed up in faith, love, and the hope of salvation. —1 Thessalonians 5:4–8 MSG

He went to church, and walked about the streets, and watched the people hurrying to and fro, and patted children on the head, and questioned beggars, and looked down into the kitchens of houses, and up to the windows; and found that everything could yield him pleasure. He had never dreamed that any walk—that anything—could give him so much happiness. —Charles Dickens, A Christmas Carol[1]

I t's Christmas Eve. You load the last of the dishes into the dishwasher, turn off the lights, and crawl into bed. Your eyelids suddenly feel extra heavy and you fall into a deep sleep. You awake the next morning—Christmas morning—in heaven. Peace and joy flood your soul. The brightness of God's glory heals you from life's wounds, *instantly*. You feel a burst of energy. You look up and wonder about the vast crowd coming your way. Then, somehow you know; this is your welcoming committee, throngs of believers who've been impacted by your life.

The people shout and cheer and give praise to God for your arrival. A young woman steps forward, warmly grabs your shoulders, looks deep into your eyes with smiling gratitude, and says, "I'm here because of you. I grew up in

Guatemala. I met a young man one day at a watering hole. He told me about Jesus. He was on a mission trip with his youth group. You gave generously so he could make that trip." She then turns around and waves forward some of her family members—parents, siblings, and cousins. She smiles widely and says, "We're all here because of you."

You had no idea. None whatsoever. You lose track of time listening to stories from people from all over the world who, one by one, share intimate details of how your life and your stewardship impacted their eternity. With one hand on your heart and the other over your mouth, you're speechless. What you considered a Christian duty, or an insignificant act, turned out to be a supernatural transaction of the most sacred kind. For the briefest moment you wish you had lived all in, believing that God truly moves on every act prompted by your faith.

You hear the dog bark, and you suddenly wake up to your actual life. Still under the covers, you feel a catch in your throat. You've been given another chance to invest your whole life in the coming kingdom. You shudder when you think of your natural bent to live as if this life is all there is. But you know better now. You know the truth. There's a kingdom that's coming. And how you live here directly impacts how you'll arrive and thrive there.

But on the judgment day, fire will reveal what kind of work each builder has done. The fire will show if a person's work has any value. If the work survives, that builder will receive a reward. But if the work is burned up, the builder will suffer great loss. The builder will be saved, but like someone barely escaping through a wall of flames.

1 Corinthians 3:13–15

Jesus told this parable to His disciples:

"There was a certain rich man who had a manager handling his affairs. One day a report came that the manager was wasting his employer's money. So the employer called him in and said, 'What's this I hear about you? Get your report in order, because you are going to be fired.'

"The manager thought to himself, 'Now what? My boss has fired me. I don't have strength to dig ditches, and I'm too proud to beg. Ah, I know how to ensure that I'll have plenty of friends who will give me a home when I am fired.'"

Luke 16:1–4

This man invited each person who owed his employer money to discuss his situation. He reduced the amount owed and collected immediately on each of these accounts. Jesus continued with His analogy:

"The rich man had to admire the dishonest rascal for being so shrewd. And it is true that the children of this world are more shrewd in dealing with the world around them than are the children of the light. Here's the lesson: Use your worldly resources to benefit others and make friends. Then, when your possessions are gone, they will welcome you to an eternal home."

Luke 16:8–9

Jesus obviously wasn't condoning dishonest behavior. He used such a drastic illustration to teach His followers that the people of this world shouldn't be better at stewarding opportunities than the people of His kingdom. Over and over again, Jesus used parables to teach about stewardship when it comes to the eternal kingdom. He wants us to think now about our eternal future and the friends who will be there waiting to welcome us home. Our worldly possessions will one day return to dust, and what will we have to show for it all? The friends we've introduced to Jesus who will one day welcome us home.

This shrewd man knew he was about to be fired and thought only of himself. In contrast, Jesus charges us to use every opportunity in front of us—our time, our finances, our special talents—to bring people into the kingdom.

In Dickens' *A Christmas Carol*, we read about a miserly, wealthy man named Ebenezer Scrooge. He didn't care about God and he didn't care about people. As a result, he made himself and others miserable. Then one night, he was visited by the ghost of his former business partner, Jacob Marley, and the ghosts of Christmas past, present, and future.

Scrooge was given a front-row seat to see the impact of a self-made, selfish life. Once he realized how deeply his choices impacted the present and future for others, he awoke to become a kind and generous man.

To be shrewd is to be sharp, astute, and able to discern an opportunity when you see one. To be a scrooge is to disregard people, responsibility, and future impact. We might not be as miserably snarky as Scrooge, but we're easily as selfish when we live as if this life, our comforts, and our possessions are all that matter.

We can spend all of our Christmas budget on giving gifts to those who are already rich, and they may forget about them by February. Or we can strategically use some of our time, treasures, and talents to help the hurting and to creatively point people to Jesus and to His coming kingdom.

Scrooge found happiness after he learned to give it away. It will be the same with us. Why? Because we are created in the image of God and it's in His nature to give. He loved us so much that He gave us His Son. He loves us so much that He sends us new mercies every morning. He loves us so much that He forgives and forgives again. He loves us so much that He takes the smallest seed sown and turns it into a harvest of righteousness. He *wants* to reward our faith. He intends to multiply our offerings. This Christmas, may you know the radical joy that comes from living an intentional kingdom life.

Prepare Him Room

King Jesus, You've made Your heart perfectly clear. I'm not sure why I miss it so easily. You care about the lost, the hurting, and the broken. You came to heal broken hearts, bind up their wounds, and save their souls, just as You've done for me. Forgive me for being so wrapped up in my own story that I miss the bigger story You're writing on the earth today. I want to be creative, innovative, and profoundly generous for Your name's sake. I want to steward opportunities with an otherworldly wisdom from above. Help me to live like Your promises are true. I'm just passing through, on my way to live forever with You. Amen.

Look Up

Fast this Christmas from the need to impress the already rich with gifts you cannot afford. Give good gifts. But remember the poor. Remember the kingdom. Rise up this season and look for creative ways to fund the kingdom (e.g., give a year-end gift to a ministry, purchase Bibles to give away, help a struggling family). Live with eternity in mind.

LIVE LIKE JESUS

Today's Reading: Luke 17

OTHER PASSAGES TO PONDER

God blesses those whose hearts are pure, for they will see God. —Matthew 5:8

> Who may climb the mountain of the LORD?
>   Who may stand in his holy place?
> Only those whose hands and hearts are pure,
>   who do not worship idols
>   and never tell lies. —Psalm 24:3–4

How would things change if you resolved to rebel against your own indifference and embody the things you long to see in the world? If you resolved that you would pursue beauty and resist brokenness? That you would resist idolatry with worship, exhaustion with rest, apathy with hunger, fear with hospitality, contempt with honor, hate with love, privilege with sacrifice, and cynicism with celebration? —Jon Tyson[1]

Jesus left Galilee for the last time with His eyes fixed on Jerusalem. You can almost picture His focused, purposeful gaze. He still had much to teach His followers. Some of His lessons were hard to understand and would only make sense in hindsight. For example (from the previous chapter), a distracted listener might think he heard Jesus compliment a crook when it seems He should have scolded him. Jesus was actually calling His people to leverage every opportunity for the kingdom, for that is why He came and that is why we're alive on the earth in this moment.

The lessons in today's chapter might cause the casual follower to drop back and follow someone with a more upbeat message. But Jesus didn't come to entertain us. He came to save us.

Luke chapter seventeen is for the serious follower of Christ—the one who believes that Jesus is indeed the hope of the world and that His ways lead to life eternally and abundantly. Consider today's chapter a bootcamp for the soul.

Heroic men and women who join the armed forces do so knowing that they'll have authority only when they're under authority. They fully expect bootcamp to break them of their bad attitudes and habits and train them in the ways of strategy and warfare. Likewise, we have a very real enemy whose aim is to steal, kill, and destroy. Jesus unapologetically goes after the attitudes in our lives that He knows will destroy us or that will give the enemy easy access to us. A casual approach to sin, a willingness to hold a grudge, and an entitled and ungrateful heart all leave a wide-open door for the enemy to walk in and sabotage our lives. Besides, we're called to something so much higher, so much greater than our natural default to sin and selfishness.

Let's go back to the bootcamp analogy. Servicemen and women are trained to take orders, to work together, and to understand enemy warfare. They know that once bootcamp is over, their first assignment may take them behind enemy lines.

In a similar fashion, Jesus' teaching in this chapter prepares us to navigate life on earth, behind enemy lines, while we wait for Him to return for us. He asks nothing from us that He hasn't already done for us.

> *We're called to something so much higher, so much greater than our natural default to sin and selfishness.*

Jesus stood up from His throne, took off His kingly robe, and broke through the cosmos to enter the womb of a teenage girl. The star shone bright that first Christmas night. The heavens watched as Jesus entered our world on a rescue mission. Creation held its breath as Jesus made Himself known for the sake of the lost, the hurting, and the broken. Wise men sought Him then and wise men still seek Him today.

Our Savior placed Himself behind enemy lines. Was willing to be associated with outcasts and sinners. Took on a religious establishment that made fellowship with God seem almost impossible. Jesus was routinely insulted, mocked, set up, and harassed. And He endured a horrific, traumatic, unjust execution.

Yet, He walked through life with a pure, humble, strong, and loving heart. He never held a grudge. Never wasted a moment. And continually forgave those who sent Him to the cross. Love motivated His every step.

We have access to the same power that raised Jesus from the grave!

The disciples surely scratched their heads though as they listened to Jesus' seemingly impossible standard for them. In their eye-for-an-eye culture, Jesus shocks them with this charge:

> "So watch yourselves! If another believer sins, rebuke that person; then if there is repentance, forgive. Even if that person wrongs you seven times a day and each time turns again and asks forgiveness, you must forgive."

> Luke 17:3–4

I'm quite sure I would have responded the way the disciples did. They simply said, *"Increase our faith!"* They knew they didn't yet have a heart like His. Hard to forgive once, let alone repeatedly. Challenging to confront another sinner, especially while maintaining a pure and humble heart. *"Increase our faith!"* they prayed. Jesus urged them to act upon the faith they already possessed. Even a little faith in action accomplishes great and powerful things. Jesus showed them the high standard of holiness and then reminded them of the supernatural power at work on their behalf.

From there, Jesus addressed entitlement and ingratitude, both of which will poison the soul. Again, picture Jesus, with all of the love in His heart, preparing the disciples He loved to prevail on the earth for the sake of the kingdom. When Jesus talked about their duty to serve without expecting reward, He wasn't contradicting what He said in Luke chapter twelve. It's still true that when He returns, if He finds us serving Him faithfully, He *promises* to put on an apron, seat us at the banqueting table, and serve *us*. Imagine! What Jesus warns against in today's chapter is the entitled attitude that creeps into our hearts when we work hard for Him.

Here again, Jesus reminds us that whatever attitude we allow in our hearts will directly impact the way we serve Him and love others. This is why we must continually give time and space to the Holy Spirit to guide, guard, correct, and redirect. And it's why we must be profoundly intentional about what we allow in and what we keep out of our hearts.

Watch over your heart with all diligence,
For from it flow the springs of life.
Put away from you a deceitful (lying, misleading)
    mouth,
And put devious lips far from you.
Let your eyes look directly ahead [toward the path
    of moral courage]
And let your gaze be fixed straight in front of you
    [toward the path of integrity].
Consider well and watch carefully the path of your
    feet,
And all your ways will be steadfast and sure.
Do not turn away to the right nor to the left [where
    evil may lurk];
Turn your foot from [the path of] evil.

                                    Proverbs 4:23–27 AMP

The more Christlike you become, the more credibility you will have in the true kingdom of God. Jesus doesn't look at the outward appearance; He sees, knows, and discerns our hearts. He deeply loves you. He's profoundly equipped you. And He's called you to shine your light so brightly that it dispels the darkness around you. His light now shines in your heart to light the way for those wandering in darkness to find their way to Him.

Jesus wants to train and transform you to such a degree that you learn to thrive behind enemy lines, know how to stand in battle, know how to rest under His wing, and know how to trust His love in an increasingly unloving world. Jesus wants to lead you on the path of healing, restoration, and renewal. And He wants you sober, alert, and ready for His return. The end of the world as we know it is serious business. And we're closer to that day than ever before. The masses will be caught up in life as usual when God shows up and puts a period at the end of His sentence. People won't be ready for it. Won't at all be prepared. But Jesus wants you to live ready.

PREPARE HIM ROOM

Father in heaven, I can be such an earthbound traveler at times. I'm so aware of my default settings when it comes to sin, selfishness, and other people's faults. Forgive me, Lord. Transform me, Father. Make me into the person You always dreamed I could be. Open my spiritual eyes to the reality of Your kingdom. Give me a heart to discern truth from lie, right from wrong, and love from hate. Remove my taste for lesser things that I might be focused solely on Your coming kingdom. This earth will soon pass away. I want You to find me ready, faithful, and grateful. I love You, Lord. Amen.

Look Up

Fast from all negative, cynical, critical attitudes this season. Just say no to them. Do the hard work of forgiveness. Entrust the people and the details to God. If you've earned the right to speak into someone's life, and that someone is wandering into sin, prayerfully make a plan to sit down and have a loving conversation with them. You're in training. You're equipped. God is with you.

DO YOU KNOW HIM?

Today's Reading: Luke 18

OTHER PASSAGES TO PONDER

Jesus replied, "If you only knew the gift God has for you and who you are speaking to, you would ask me, and I would give you living water." —John 4:10

> Yes, the Sovereign LORD is coming in power.
>> He will rule with a powerful arm.
>> See, he brings his reward with him as he comes.
>>> —Isaiah 40:10

He guards, and He guides. He heals the sick. He cleanses the lepers. He forgives sinners. He discharges debtors. He delivers the captives. He defends the feeble.

He blesses the young. He serves the unfortunate. He regards the aged.
He rewards the diligent, and He beautifies the meek.
Now, that's my King. Do you know Him? —S. M. Lockridge[1]

M y birthday falls exactly one week before Christmas. Hard to compete with Jesus.☺ For some reason, I feel all kinds of tension and vulnerability around my birthday. It's a busy time for everyone. I never want to inconvenience anyone's already busy schedule. Plus, I'm an introvert. Still, there's a piece of me that wants to be celebrated, even though I may end up hiding in the bathroom the whole time.

I remember one year amidst the Christmas season, it occurred to me that there were no family plans on the calendar for my birthday. I asked my dear husband about it, and I could tell by the look on his face that though he hadn't forgotten about my birthday, the time had slipped away, and we'd have to scramble to put something together. I felt like an afterthought, an inconvenience. It's embarrassing to admit this now, but I broke down and cried. This seemingly trivial pain stirred up some deeper hurts buried in my soul. Our conversation escalated, and I said something I shouldn't have. The pain in my husband's eyes put a knot in my gut. He leaned in and asked, *"Do you even know me?"* Gulp.

Truth is, I know him well. He's one of the most grounded, stable, strong, and kind men on the planet. He'd made an honest mistake. It's sad how easily circumstances can skew our perspective and make us doubt what we know to be true.

As we walk through Luke chapter eighteen, we find a reason to ask ourselves, *Do we even know who Jesus is? Do we know how He is? Do we place more weight on our ever-shaking circumstances than we do on His unshakable character? Are we still more confident in our ability to get it right than we are in the fact that He is always right and always good?*

One day Jesus told His disciples a story to show that they should *always* pray and *never* give up. Jesus described a poor widow who suffered injustice and needed an advocate. This dear woman's circumstances placed her at a severe disadvantage. She was a woman (not recognized in a court of law), and she was poor (had no means to pay for her defense). Yet, she was relentless and would not be denied!

Why did this destitute woman have to appeal to a judge who neither feared God nor cared about people? Jesus used this story as a great example of how to pray and not give up. I wrote a whole book on that topic.[2] But let's zoom out a bit and consider the contrast between the unrighteous judge and our righteous and holy God.

Do we know Him? If an unrighteous judge would eventually hand out justice, won't God Himself come to our aid, stand in our defense, and answer our prayers when the time is right? This parable, in some ways, is a lesson in contrasts. The widow was poor, was without an advocate, and stood before an ungodly judge. We, as heirs of God, on the other hand,

- are recognized in the heavenly court and have every right to appear before the King; furthermore, we can be assured of His glad welcome (Ephesians 3:12; Hebrews 4:16). . . .
- have an advocate—Jesus Himself. He intercedes for us day and night. We're not bending the ear of an unrighteous judge to get his attention (1 John 2:1; Hebrews 7:25). . . .
- have the heart and the ear of our God, who longs for us, loves us, and intends to finish what He started in us (Psalm 18:6; Philippians 1:6).[3]

We approach Jesus with assurance and confidence not because we're perfect, but because He is. We fully trust that He'll come through for us because of who He is, how He is, and how He has grafted us into His family. We cannot perform well enough to earn a miracle for our families, finances, or health.

We approach Jesus with assurance and confidence not because we're perfect, but because He is.

Jesus wrapped up this parable with an important question:

"But when the Son of Man returns, how many will he find on the earth who have faith?"

Luke 18:8

The word *faith* in this passage translates this way: *The conviction that God exists and is the creator and ruler of all things, the provider and bestower of eternal salvation through Christ.* Two words related to *faith* are *fidelity* and *faithfulness*, which mean *having confidence in the character of the one who can be relied on.*[4]

Let's sit with that idea for a moment. Jesus not only invites us into a relationship that involves audacious and tenacious prayer, but He's also asking us to remember who it is we're talking to. We genuinely are tethered to a good, good God who remembers our birthday, collects our tears, heals our hurts, and defends us against our soul's enemy. He intervenes in our situation, leads us when we're unaware, and establishes us in His purposes. He softens the hardest hearts, forgives the worst of sinners, and uses the most unlikely saints to accomplish His purposes on the earth. This is our God.

We're not journeying through this life like a rudderless ship or with a sail flapping in the wind. We have a purpose. We were created by God Himself, and He knows our name, where we live, and what stresses us out from day to day. We serve a sovereign, overseeing, holy, and good-good King. *Do you know Him?*

Two men went to the temple to pray. One was a Pharisee and one was a despised tax collector. The Pharisee wasn't really praying; he was pontificating—bragging, really. He showed up to show off. On the other hand, the tax collector knew full well that his own humanity disqualified him if not for the mercy and grace of God. One man approached God expecting praise, the other, hoping for mercy.

Jesus' response?

"I tell you, this sinner, not the Pharisee, returned home justified before God. For those who exalt themselves will be humbled, and those who humble themselves will be exalted."

Luke 18:14

Here again, we're invited to observe the difference between one who knows God and one who does not. Someone once said, "When you feel too big for your own britches, go stand before a vast ocean and remember that its Creator easily holds those waters in His hand."

Have you noticed how easy it is to strike up your own defense? To judge someone else who does the very things that you do but maybe to a higher degree? Why do we do that? I submit it's because we've forgotten who God is.

When I catch myself noticing someone who spends too much money or who squanders their time, and I'm tempted to feel a bit better about myself for not spending *that* much money or for not wasting *that* much time, I have to ask myself, *Do you really want to go there?* Do I want to put myself before a Most Holy God and strike my own defense? Have I forgotten who it is that forgave me, saved me, and redeemed me?

People who've walked with God a long time and know Him for who He is would rather swim in His ocean of grace than stand on their flimsy attempt at righteousness. Every personal flaw we're forced to acknowledge, the frustration we face, the hurt we feel, and the delays we endure beg the question, *Do we know Him?*

We tend to think that if we get our immediate needs met, and if people don't disappoint us, and if our plans turn out the way we hope they will, life will be good and we will be okay. But it's just not true. The whole purpose of our lives is to know God more, walk in His way, and trust His nature.

Jesus wants to know that when He returns, He'll find faith—a confident and sound hope in His character—*in our hearts*. We don't acquire that kind of confidence overnight. We come by it one faith-choice at a time. It's impossible to please God without faith. And it's impossible to trust someone you do not know and love. *Do you know Him?*

> I bow before your holy Temple as I worship.
>> I praise your name for your unfailing love and
>>> faithfulness;
>> for your promises are backed
>>> by all the honor of your name.
>
> Psalm 138:2

Prepare Him Room

King of kings, Lord of lords, I bow before You this day and honor You for who You are. Forgive me for being so easily shaken by my circumstances. Help me to know You more. You are sovereign, You are good, You are kind, and You are true. You are faithful, and You love me. If I could see You in all of Your glory and strength, looking at me with eyes of great love and affection, I'd confidently face my foes without wavering, knowing You'd be there for me. Help me to trust that's true even now. I am Yours, and You are mine. What a glorious reality! Amen.

Look Up

Make it your aim to know God more. Seek His face. Read His Word. Listen for His voice. Fiercely fast from the temptation to judge others. Avoid like the plague any tendency to engage in prideful self-praise. Humble yourself before Almighty God. He will lift you up and establish you before a watching world.

An Unexpected Savior

Today's Reading: Luke 19

Other Passages to Ponder

The stone that the builders rejected has now become
the cornerstone.
This is the LORD's doing, and it is wonderful to see.
  —Psalm 118:22–23

Rejoice, O people of Zion! Shout in triumph, O people
of Jerusalem!
Look, your king is coming to you. He is righteous and
victorious,
yet he is humble, riding on a donkey—riding on a
donkey's colt. —Zechariah 9:9

Today, fast spiritual spectatorship. Enter into worship. When considerations start turning into hesitations about something Jesus is clearly at the center of, throw hypercaution to the wind, and celebrate Jesus with abandon. —Alicia Britt Chole[1]

There's a picture in a pile of old family photos that's worth a thousand words. I'm about six years old, my brother, about seven and a half. We're sitting in front of the Christmas tree with our newly opened gifts. Me with my new doll and my brother Jeff with his GI Joe truck. Only one of us is smiling. Jeff grins ear to ear; he holds up his truck with two hands like it is the best thing since sliced bread. I hold my doll by the hair and let her dangle in the air. I refused to smile for the camera because I was soooo disappointed in my gift. I was a tomboy through and through and didn't want a girly gift for Christmas.

My mom found my angst so funny that she decided to capture it on film. I didn't see the humor at the time. We laugh about it now. It took me a while to admit it, but I eventually fell in love with that doll. Over the years my mom not only checked a few things off of our Christmas lists that we wanted, but she also surprised us with gifts that we didn't ask for but ended up loving most of all.

Over and over, Jesus disrupted the status quo. The Jewish people expected one thing and Jesus gave them another. They expected Him to make His grand entrance with pomp and circumstance, but He entered the world through the womb of a poor, teenage girl. They expected a powerful king that would overthrow Rome. Instead, they got a humble servant who *suffered and died* for His people. And, consequently, whose resurrection victory *overthrew the very powers of hell*. They expected a king who'd abide by the law and maintain social distance from those who'd made a real mess of their lives. Instead, they got a King who broke tradition and yet fulfilled the law, and who crossed social barriers to reach the messy, hurting, humble heart.

Jesus continually frustrated those with rigid expectations, yet He delighted those who expected nothing but at times dared to hope for something.

Before getting to Jerusalem, Jesus stopped at Jericho. Zacchaeus, a notorious sinner and chief tax collector, shimmied up a tree to get a better look at the man who was the talk of the town. To Zacchaeus' great delight, Jesus smiled at him and invited Himself to dinner. Once again, expectations blown to smithereens. Jesus enjoyed food, laughter, and rich conversation with a group of thieves most everyone despised. He knew this move would upset many, yet He did it anyway. Not for the sake of disruption but for the sake of a heart ready to receive his King. Zacchaeus and his friends were thrilled. Others, aghast; they gossiped and grumbled their way through the crowd. Jesus didn't always do what the people wanted Him to do, but He did what the world needed Him to do. He took His cues from the Father and saved souls, one at a time. While at Zacchaeus' house, Jesus declared:

> "Salvation has come to this home today, for this man has shown himself to be a true son of Abraham. For the Son of Man came to seek and save those who are lost."
>
> Luke 19:9–10

Like Him or not, people wanted to hear what Jesus had to say. Next, He told the parable of the king's ten servants. He did so *to correct the impression that the kingdom of God would begin right away* (see v. 11). Once again, people assumed that once the Messiah made His appearance, culture and systems would change practically overnight. And permanently. No more Roman oppression. There was a new king in town. But instead, Jesus explained that the crowned King would arrive, but then He'd go away for a while. And His servants would be assigned the task of stewarding the kingdom until His return. What? He's not staying? And when He returns, He'll take inventory of how *we* stewarded the first phase of His coming kingdom? *Not* what people expected.

Next, fulfilling a prophecy, Jesus rode into Jerusalem on a donkey to the shouts and praises of the people:

"Blessings on the King who comes in the name of the LORD! Peace in heaven, and glory in highest heaven!"

Luke 19:38

The people had no idea how prophetic their praises were. But Jesus knew full well that those very praises would soon turn into curses. Yet He stayed on mission. As Jesus drew closer to Jerusalem, His passion surged for the city, for the lost, and especially for those with hearts so hard, they'd never admit to needing a Savior. He was so moved by their lostness that He broke down and cried. Imagine.

Who is this Man that the wind and the waves obey Him? That children are inexplicably drawn to Him? That the poorest of the poor and the marginalized adore Him? That demons flee because of Him? That leprosy is no match for Him? That sinners want to spend time with Him? That the rigid religious would despise Him enough to kill Him? And that His closest friends and followers would rather die than deny Him?

Who is this Man that the wind and the waves obey Him? That children are inexplicably drawn to Him?

Jesus is still surprising people today. Has He bewildered and astonished you as He has me? I can't count the number of times when I, much like Mary and Martha, felt that Jesus waited too long to come to my aid. My dreams died. Heartbroken, I wondered where

He was and if He cared, only to later learn that He was there all along, waiting for me to discern His presence when all I felt was His absence. Jesus taught me this unexpected lesson: While He cares deeply about the desires of our hearts (and is tending to some of those even now), any gift from His hand pales in comparison to the treasure of knowing His heart. His heartbreaking delays sent my roots deeper into the soil of His love, which proved to be a far more substantial gain than my temporary desire.

I've been startled by His unexpected goodness in moments when I was only focused on my predictable badness. I've been amazed by His mercy when I knew I deserved judgment. I've been astounded by His faithfulness when I've only given Him a few seeds of feeble faith.

Over and over, Jesus shows Himself to be strong and gentle, patient and powerful, tried and true.

Over and over, Jesus shows Himself to be strong and gentle, patient and powerful, tried and true. He doesn't belong in a box, and He's not bound by formulas. He is the King of an everlasting kingdom, and we are His joint heirs. He promised we'd have trouble in this life, but He calls us to be of good cheer because He's already overcome, which means we will overcome.

PREPARE HIM ROOM

King Jesus, You are beyond my imagination and beyond my comprehension. I want to know You more! I confess that my expectations of how I think You should show up have kept me from seeing You for who You are. You are not predictable, but You are faithful and always will be. Blow the doors off of my limiting beliefs and increase my capacity to walk with You on Your terms. Show up in my life in unexpected ways. Surprise me, Lord. Amen.

LOOK UP

Fast this holiday season from rigid expectations. But be wide open to divine surprises and setups. Open your hands and dare to pray, "Surprise me, Lord."

Day 20

LIVE, DON'T WATCH

Today's Reading: Luke 20

*Somewhere a snake hisses and a Savior on a cross declares, "It is
finished." A single red drop falls to the ground. The curtain splits
and the curse breaks and the promise of Eden comes back to us. All*

the sisters and the daughters and the mamas say, "Amen." —Holley Gerth[1]

She scrolls through her social media feed and feels her soul deflate by the moment. She gazes at the pristine homes, artfully filtered family photos, and fun Christmas outings. She sets down her phone and picks up the remote to watch another Hallmark Christmas show. She holds the carton of ice cream close and scoops up another mouthful. She looks up at her TV and wonders, *Where do they find all of these gorgeous people and gorgeous homes? And who decorates every nook and cranny of every room? Why don't my streets have lights, and wreaths, and carolers in the snow?* She sinks farther into her old couch and looks around at her dilapidated life, which is really a beautiful life, but she just can't see it at the moment. She stares off into space and recalls a recent conflict with a friend. Her stomach knots up and her anxieties rise. Why does life have to be so hard?

She rises early in the morning, grabs a cup of coffee, and settles into her favorite spot by the tree. She puts on an instrumental worship playlist and sets her phone aside. With a fire in the fireplace and a warm cup in her hand, she opens up her Bible on her lap and asks God to speak through His

Word to the deepest parts of who she is. She lays out her plans for the day and asks for wisdom and direction. God whispers the name of a neighbor walking through a difficult time. She makes a note to reach out later today. Her mind wanders to her endless task list, but she pulls her thoughts to the present and focuses on the Word before her:

> If you are wise and understand God's ways, prove it by living an honorable life, doing good works with the humility that comes from wisdom. But if you are bitterly jealous and there is selfish ambition in your heart, don't cover up the truth with boasting and lying. For jealousy and selfishness are not God's kind of wisdom. Such things are earthly, unspiritual, and demonic. For wherever there is jealousy and selfish ambition, there you will find disorder and evil of every kind.
>
> James 3:13–16

She lets the Word penetrate her heart. *Jealousy opens the door to every kind of evil?* How often she's tempted to misjudge those who have what she longs for. But she fears God and loves what she has with Him. She knows too how it feels to be on the receiving end of jealousy and wrong assumptions. She bows her head, opens her hands, humbles herself, and asks God to do a fresh work in her. *Help me to live honorably, Lord. Help me not to spend my life watching others from the sidelines. You've given me a good life and a great work to steward. I refuse to waste my time as a jealous spectator. I'm loved and equipped, and I*

*have important things to do. Help me to do them well for
Your glory. Amen.*

———————

Jesus was continually surrounded by people who were jealous of Him, who were threatened by Him, and who hoped to trap Him. Picture the religious leaders standing in the shadows, listening to Jesus. They clench their jaws, narrow their eyes, and whisper among themselves, *This man must be stopped.* One day, while He was teaching the people and preaching the good news in the temple, the leading priests and elders approached Him and demanded to know by what authority He did the things He did.

Up until this point, the Jewish people thought the Pharisees were the religious standard of the day (even though there was much corruption behind the scenes). Status was prime real estate for the Pharisees. Their power-grabbing schemes worked until they didn't. True status arrived in the form of holiness, humility, and help for the hurting. God suddenly seemed accessible. And the religious leaders found this "good news" a terrible threat to their claimed territory. If only they had been seekers instead of watchers.

Posturing for an opportunity to upend Jesus' influence, the leaders sent spies pretending to be honest men. They tried to bait Jesus into saying something that could be reported to the Roman governor so he would arrest Jesus. "Teacher," they said, "we know that you speak and teach what is right and are not influenced by what others think. You teach the way of God truthfully."[2] They hoped to trap Jesus with a question. They didn't realize they were completely outmatched. In fact, what they said in the moment about Jesus was true, even though they spoke from corrupt, cold hearts.

Jesus didn't shrink back from difficult conversations. He engaged with wisdom and insight, all the while remembering who He was. The religious leaders, on the other hand, had rested on their laurels for too long. When Jesus arrived on the scene, their own jealousy blinded them from truly seeing what God was up to in their midst. Our jealousy will do the very same thing to us. If we want to walk in God's power, we need to reflect His heart.

If we want to walk in God's power, we need to reflect His heart.

The Pharisees watched, assessed, and judged from the sidelines. Their hearts fossilized along with their sense of expectancy. The Scriptures they claimed to know so well prophesied of a coming Messiah. But they'd stopped looking expectantly for Him and instead searched for ways to kill Him.

When we live in the shadows and spend any of our precious time jealously watching others, we weaken ourselves and our influence. In due time, our spiritual muscles sag and our hearts grow cold. Imagine opening your door in the dead of a Minnesota winter and letting the frigid cold air into your toasty-warm home.

This is not to say we shouldn't watch others. In biblical times, an apprentice actually moved in with his master so he could learn his master's craft, his rhythm, and how to live an integrated life. It's not that we watch, it's *who* we watch that determines the course of our lives.

If you determine not to look to the left or right, but you instead set your face like flint and follow wholeheartedly after Jesus, you may notice a few things, like the power that infuses your steps and encourages your heart. The wisdom that comes from above when you need it most. The correction that you grow to count on because you know you're a work in progress. And the love and mercy that spills out of the Father's heart for you because you're His.

Something else will rise up too: the jealousies of others. There are those who live life powerfully and those who watch others jealously. Don't be deterred by your critics or discouraged by your doubters. They'll have to explain themselves to God one day. You be you. You do you. And you, remember that when you fix your eyes on Jesus—the author and the finisher of your faith—you will live in a way that gets both heaven's and hell's attention.

> *Don't be deterred by your critics or discouraged by your doubters. They'll have to explain themselves to God one day.*

Stay grounded in the things of God. Keep listening for His voice. Seek peace and pursue it. And leave the agitators to

God. You have a powerful life to live, and with God's help, you will.

Prepare Him Room

King Jesus, I marvel at the way You lived Your life. You stayed on mission. Handled Your critics. And helped the hurting. And though the needs were endless, You found time to slip away and enjoy some solitude in the presence of Your Father. You spoke with precision and prayed with power. With wisdom and humility You submitted to Your Father and You silenced Your critics. You weren't soft, You were tender. You weren't weak, You were yielded. You weren't absent, You were present. Help me to live like You lived. I'm following hard after You. Love You, Lord. Amen.

Look Up

Fast from "watching" in a way that weakens you. Turn off the TV, turn away from social media, and turn your eyes upward to the one who loves your soul. Read a biography about someone who inspires you. Steward your perspective with vision and wisdom.

Day 21

DISCERN THE TIMES

Today's Reading: Luke 21

OTHER PASSAGES TO PONDER

The end of the world is coming soon. Therefore, be earnest and disciplined in your prayers. Most important of all, continue to show deep love for each other, for love covers a multitude of sins. Cheerfully share your home with those who need a meal or a place to stay. —1 Peter 4:7–9

Be on guard. Stand firm in the faith. Be courageous. Be strong. And do everything with love. —1 Corinthians 16:13–14

"I'm not looking for signs," said the late Vance Havner; "I'm listening for a sound."

The sound of the trumpet! The shout of the archangel!

"Even so, come, Lord Jesus!" —The Wiersbe Bible Commentary[1]

Hunched over with an aching back and sore feet, she shuffled across the temple floor and made her way to the Court of Women. People brushed past her as if she didn't exist. The other women ignored her completely. Jesus stood off in the distance and smiled with great affection. He tapped His brother's arm and said, "Watch and learn." She made her way forward to bring her offering. She dropped in two small coins. They were so light, they barely made a sound. She gave the smallest of the Roman coins, worth about six minutes of wages.

Jesus turned to His disciples and said:

> "I tell you the truth . . . this poor widow has given more than all the rest of them. For they have given a tiny part of their surplus, but she, poor as she is, has given everything she has."

Luke 21:3–4

Jesus honored this widow's gift. By all earthly standards her offering was inconsequential. From heaven's point of view, it exceeded all of the other gifts combined. Dr. Warren Wiersbe writes, "When it comes to our giving, God sees more than *portion*; He also sees the *proportion*. Men see *what is given*, but God sees *what is left*, and by that He measures the gift and the condition of our hearts."[2] More and more, Jesus worked to wean His followers from man's opinion and from how things appear to the natural eye—a lesson for us to more deeply appreciate the eternal value of every moment of our lives.

Jesus knew His time on earth was coming to a close, and He intentionally prepared His followers for their days ahead. Once again, He reaffirmed the distinction between earthly appearances and spiritual realities.

How wise of Jesus to preface a difficult message with such a beautiful, simple example of all-in faith. This seemingly insignificant, poor widow gained heaven's attention. Such a good reminder that God sees our hearts and joyfully receives what we lovingly offer Him.

Jesus then talked about difficult times in the days ahead. Natural disasters and unexplainable weather patterns, false messiahs, betrayals, and increased persecution. And yet, through persecution, some would be brought before high-level leaders and have the chance to testify in a way they'd otherwise never get the chance to.

Jesus continues:

"And there will be strange signs in the sun, moon, and stars. And here on earth the nations will be in turmoil, perplexed by the roaring seas and strange tides. People will be terrified at what they see coming upon the earth, for the powers in the heavens will be shaken. Then everyone will see the Son of Man coming on a cloud with power and great glory. So when all these things begin to happen, stand and look up, for your salvation is near!"

Luke 21:25–28

Though we're not to try to guess the date of Christ's return, Jesus tells us to discern the times.

"When the Son of Man returns, it will be like it was in Noah's day. In those days before the flood, the people were enjoying banquets and parties and weddings right up to the time Noah entered his boat. People didn't realize what was going to happen until the flood came and swept them all away. That is the way it will be when the Son of Man comes."

Matthew 24:37–39

Two things marked Noah's day: *decadence* and *desertion.* The times were evil, and people didn't care. They partied, got drunk, numbed out, and had a good time. And they abandoned any fear of God they once had. When people turn their backs on God, wickedness flourishes, and when wickedness prospers, the vulnerable suffer. When the weak and vulnerable suffer too long, God eventually steps in.

Just the other day I was reading in the book of Jeremiah about how God had had enough with the deserters. They'd flippantly disregarded the Most High God and went so far as to mock His prophets. Called God's prophets windbags and implied that they didn't speak for God. Pretty bold, wouldn't you say? If they'd turned their backs on God, how in the world would they know who spoke for God? Read what happens next:

> Therefore, this is what the LORD God of Heaven's
>   Armies says:
> "Because the people are talking like this,
>   my messages will flame out of your mouth
>   and burn the people like kindling wood."
>
> Jeremiah 5:14

Consider this: The degree to which deserters mock God's people will be the degree to which God pours out His power on His people. God will make sure that His people will speak with courage, boldness, authority, and truth.

After all God had done for His people, the deserters had completely abandoned Him. Listen to God's passionate appeal and notice what He's looking for in us:

> "Have you no respect for me?
>   Why don't you tremble in my presence?
> I, the LORD, define the ocean's sandy shoreline
>   as an everlasting boundary that the waters
>   cannot cross.
> The waves may toss and roar,
>   but they can never pass the boundaries I set.
> But my people have stubborn and rebellious hearts.

They have turned away and abandoned me.
They do not say from the heart,
    'Let us live in awe of the LORD our God,
for he gives us rain each spring and fall,
    assuring us of a harvest when the time is right.'
Your wickedness has deprived you of these
      wonderful blessings.
    Your sin has robbed you of all these good things."

Jeremiah 5:22–25

Let's break this passage down a bit.

- God deserves our respect. He spoke the galaxies into existence and delights in every detail of our lives.
- We're called to know His holiness, majesty, and power so well that we tremble in His presence.
- We're called to be so in tune with Him and His creation that we continually stand in awe of His handiwork.
- We're invited to so enjoy our relationship with Him that we instinctively say, "Let us live in awe of the Lord our God; for He supplies our needs and brings us a harvest when the time is right."
- Certain blessings are reserved for those who walk in the fear of the Lord.

What are we to do with the difficult passages in Luke chapter twenty-one? We draw near to God. We walk in the fear of the Lord. We resist the temptations toward decadence and desertion. The farther we wander, the more sin we'll justify, and the more sin takes root in our hearts, the less God's ways will influence our lives.

God deserves our respect. He spoke the galaxies into existence and delights in every detail of our lives.

It seems we're living in days much like Noah's. People don't even care to know the truth. They want to believe what they want to believe. How then shall we live?

> This is how the LORD responds:
> "If you return to me, I will restore you
>   so you can continue to serve me.
> If you speak good words rather than worthless ones,
>   you will be my spokesman.
> You must influence them;
>   do not let them influence you!"
>
>   Jeremiah 15:19

Another translation, the NASB, reads, "If you extract the precious from the worthless, you will become My spokesman." These are difficult days, but nobody is getting away with anything. This isn't a time for decadent indulgence; it's a time for sober reflection and mountain-moving faith.

Trying to live with one foot in the kingdom and one foot out will only tear you in two. The great divide has already begun. Make no mistake about it: A great party awaits us. Celebrations galore. But not yet. Right now, Jesus asks us for our undivided attention. Look around your sphere of influence; observe your culture. To what is He calling you? Can you find something precious in the midst of poison? Can you shine your light in the darkness?

This earth will pass away. We are foreigners just passing through. This place is not our home, so we ought not try to make it so. God gives us good gifts in the land of the living. But He promised we'd suffer too. But a day is coming when He'll wipe away every tear from our eyes. Until then, we live by faith. We offer our offerings. We reach out to others in love. We hold on to hope. And we keep our eyes on the eastern sky.

Prepare Him Room

Dear Jesus, I'm tempted to be terrified of the times we're in. But I look to You. You're where my help comes from. Help me to live in a manner worthy of Your name. Help me to extract the precious from the worthless that I might be Your spokesperson. Give me faith to believe You for miracles and a heart of courage to steward them. Eternity is everything. Help me trust You in the meantime. In Jesus' name, I pray. Amen.

LOOK UP

Fast from indulgences that you know weaken you. Ask God to show you where and how you've let your guard down and compromised your faith. Use this beautiful holiday to reconnect with your Savior.

Day 22

COMMUNION

Today's Reading: Luke 22

But he was pierced for our rebellion, crushed for our
sins.
He was beaten so we could be whole. He was whipped
so we could be healed. —Isaiah 53:5

For I pass on to you what I received from the Lord himself.
On the night when he was betrayed, the Lord Jesus took
some bread and gave thanks to God for it. Then he broke it
in pieces and said, "This is my body, which is given for you.
Do this in remembrance of me." —1 Corinthians 11:23–24

How many times do you suppose that night was replayed in the minds of the disciples? Did the impact of Jesus' actions have an increasingly greater place in their lives as they grew in faith over the years? —Susie Larson[1]

Though His betrayal was in motion, Jesus served *Communion*. He reclined at the table in the presence of His enemy. Jesus knew that in a few short hours He would face rejection, torture, and execution. And with the longing and passion of His humble heart, He looked forward to getting His disciples around the table for the sake of Communion.

Before His followers had a chance to be traumatized by the devil's evil schemes, Jesus put a flag in the ground. He essentially said to them, "*Remember this. Remember us.* Remember that the enemy hasn't taken My

> *Though His betrayal was in motion, Jesus served Communion.*

life; I have freely given it. Remember that though your badness once disqualified you, the Father's goodness has saved you. *This* is the new covenant. Remember that though I am well aware of what lies ahead of me on that cross, My deepest desire beforehand is to be with you, break bread with you, and remind you that My promises are true. Though schemes are being devised behind My back, I want you, My beloved ones, to see My face." Oh, the love of Jesus.

I just can't get this phrase out of my mind: "*On the night He was betrayed*, He took the bread and broke it, saying this is My body, given up for *you*." As if that night was one seamless Kingly piece of fabric, Jesus served, loved, and amidst the plan against His life, reminded us to remember Him.

Outside, the soldiers were receiving their orders to find and capture a rebel. Inside, the King of the universe was preparing to go to the Cross. Empty accusations. Kingdom response.[2]

One day, author and pastor's wife Kay Warren joined me on my radio show. She shared this insight with our listeners (my paraphrase): "During our time this side of heaven, our joy will always be accompanied by some kind of sorrow. Like train tracks that run side by side, joy and sorrow are so often equally present in our lives. But one day, if you look in the distance, you'll notice how the two tracks become one, and all we'll know is joy. No more sorrow."

So often our holidays feel that way, no? A mixed bag of joys and sorrows. If we're not careful, we'll get so caught up in our momentary disappointments that we'll miss the sacred, beautiful changes taking place around us and within us.

Pay attention to your journey. God's grace is a daily provision for you. His strength is constantly at work within you. His way is a healing and maturing pilgrimage. At various times along the way (when you're ready), He'll lead you back to your painful memories so He can bring redemptive truth where destructive lies have taken up residence.

Consider Peter for a moment. He denied Christ while warming himself by a bonfire. Several scholars have noted that if not for Jesus' loving intervention, Peter would have been continually triggered and possibly traumatized every time he cooked over a charcoal fire. Think about it. Jesus had been unjustly accused, roughly taken away to be condemned, and then killed. Peter gave up everything to follow Jesus. He knew Jesus was the Messiah. Loved Him immensely. And yet when his own safety was on the line, Peter abandoned Jesus. He knew right away he'd blown it. He wept bitterly. You can be sure the enemy condemned him fiercely. How do you recover from something like that?

With Jesus you can, and you will.

After the Messiah died and rose from the grave, He appeared to many people on several different occasions. We read in John's gospel about how one day Jesus appeared to the disciples beside the Sea of Galilee. He yelled out to the disciples, "Catch any fish?" When they said no, Jesus told them to try again. This time they caught so many fish, they didn't have the strength to haul them into the boat.

These kinds of miracles don't just happen. Suddenly John's eyes were opened, and he said, "Peter, it's the Lord!"

I laugh out loud—with great joy and celebration—every time I read how Peter didn't wait for the others, didn't wait for them to paddle in their weighed-down boat. He whipped on his tunic, jumped in the water, and paddled to the shore to see his Lord. Don't you just love that scene?

Guess what Jesus had waiting for Peter on the beach? A charcoal fire. He brought Peter back to that whole sensory experience to give him a new memory. Peter stood by the warmth of the fire. He could smell the charcoal smoke, and, in that moment, he looked up and saw Jesus' love, affection, and acceptance with no hint of condemnation. Jesus grabbed Peter by the shoulders and said, "Peter, do you love Me?" For every time Peter denied Christ, he was given a new chance to affirm his love for his Savior in a setting where God's grace abounded for him. Don't you just love our Lord?

We will find ourselves, on occasion, in scenarios that seem too much for us. We'll react in ways that are beneath us. We'll be prime candidates for condemnation. Do we dig ourselves out of the hole? Talk ourselves out of our self-contempt? Not at all.

We make our way to the table of grace and we have Communion. We repent of our sins, and we look to Jesus' amazing, saving, and redemptive grace. We don't rehearse our badness. We remember His goodness. And as we walk intimately with Jesus and follow His lead throughout our life, we'll find that He sometimes brings us back to those places of failure, pain, or betrayal so we can acquire new memories of His victory, healing power, and undying acceptance.

Jesus called us to remember backward—to look back and remember what actually happened with Jesus. He died for us. Defeated death. And rose from the grave.

Yet when Jesus served Communion, He was remembering forward. He's not limited by time or space. He knew what He was about to make available to us. He knew that the impossible was about to become possible. He knew that an epic story was about to be unleashed into the world and that the gates of hell would not—could not—prevail against it! He went the distance on the cross so that we could reign with Him. Let that truth sink deep into your bones.

Do not fret if your Christmas season isn't as you hoped it would be. Rejoice that you serve a living Savior who's working even now to heal your soul and redeem every aspect of your story.

Prepare Him Room

Precious Lord, I can get so caught up in my moments of sorrow and sadness that I sometimes forget about Your goodness. You have redeemed my soul, and You're in the process of redeeming my story. I pause this day and I remember Your sacrifice, Your gift of life, and the victory You won for me on the cross. Help me to sense Your presence today. This Christmas season help me to immerse myself in thoughts of Your goodness. You have no rival. You're the King of kings. And You love me. Thank you, Lord. Amen.

LOOK UP

Fast from condemnation. Refuse to let your sorrows swallow you whole. The joy of the Lord is your strength. There's grace in this place just for you. As you walk with Jesus, you're moving forward, upward and onward to that day when every tear will be wiped away. So today, don't lose heart. Take heart and be of good cheer. Jesus has overcome the world.

Day 23

DEATH DEFEATED!

Today's Reading: Luke 23

O death, where is your victory? O death, where is your sting?
—1 Corinthians 15:55

When he ascended to the heights, he led a crowd of captives and gave gifts to his people. —Ephesians 4:8

The Lion of Judah roars, "All debts are paid. All past, present, and future claims are cancelled. Forever. . . . I have bought mankind back with My blood. My children are justified, redeemed, sanctified. No longer slaves. I have snatched them back out of the hand of the deceiver. Sin no longer has dominion. My children are no longer under law but under grace!" —Charles Martin[1]

Here we are, on the eve of Christmas Eve. Perhaps you're putting the finishing touches on a few presents or wrapping up your baked goods, anticipating a time of celebration and fun with family and friends. I'm excited for you. And it's here we find ourselves reading through the darkest day of human history: Jesus' crucifixion. Though you may be tempted to skip this one for today, let's lean into it instead. What Jesus did here, He did *for you*. What He won here, He won *for you*.

It's impossible to comprehend the freedom Jesus purchased for us if we don't first understand the depths of our own captivity. So, take a few moments with this one, will you? Remember who you were and how you were when Jesus first saved you. Consider the miracle of your salvation.

> Remember, dear brothers and sisters, that few of you were wise in the world's eyes or powerful or wealthy when God called you. Instead, God chose things the world considers foolish in order to shame those who think they are wise. And he chose things that are powerless to shame those who are powerful. God chose things despised by the world, things counted as nothing at all, and used them to bring to nothing

what the world considers important. As a result, no one can ever boast in the presence of God.

1 Corinthians 1:26–29

One of the beautiful gifts you could offer back to God this Christmas season is the gift of time and remembrance. Ponder how you've changed because of Christ's work in you. Imagine how you'd be if not for His miraculous saving work in your life. I shudder to think of how selfish and insecure I'd still be if not for the redeeming and refining work of Christ in my life. How has the living, breathing life of Christ in you changed you?

Me? I'm less insecure, more confident, and yet far humbler than I used to be (God repeatedly humbles me, but never humiliates me). I'm less afraid of the things I once feared because I'm far more acquainted with the Father's love, which has brought great assurance to my soul. I'm less selfish than I used to be and far more generous because I now know that God's storehouses are overflowing and that He always provides seed to the one who generously sows.[2] I notice and care for others first. Prior to coming to Christ, all I could see was myself, my sin, and my frailties. Maybe you've heard me say this before, but it didn't take me long to learn that insecurity is just another form of selfishness. I'm far more dependent on the Father, and far less dependent upon my own efforts to strive, prove, or accomplish things. It's God who establishes us, defines us, vindicates us, and works through us. Far more rests on His shoulders than on mine. I know that truth deeply now. Also, I think more often these days about eternity. I no longer look to this life to satisfy all of my deepest longings. I believe in God's miraculous power to intervene more than I fear the enemy's evil intent to destroy. I know now that this is not an equal fight. Jesus has no rival. He's the King. The enemy is a created being, and he has his limits. I now spend more time enjoying the Father's love and less time fearing the enemy's influence. Those are some of the ways I've changed, not by my own merit, but by the miraculous work of God within me. How about you? Do you have a few moments to sit down and consider what God has accomplished in and through you?

Give God a treasured gift this Christmas: *Marvel* that He saved you, at how He saved you, and at what this means both for your present and your future. If you think of it, it's truly quite miraculous. God literally reached down from on high and pulled you out of the kingdom of darkness and brought you into the kingdom of His dear Son, who purchased your freedom with His own life. What a wonder! He forgave all of your sins. Took away Satan's claimed territory in your life. Filled you with His Spirit. And secured your eternity. *You are in Christ and Christ is in you.* Let that sink in for a moment. The Holy Spirit has taken up residence in you and works mightily in you to change and redeem you from the inside out. You're one of God's treasured possessions. And His kingdom is coming to the earth through you. Wow. Just imagine.

We also pray that you will be strengthened with all his glorious power so you will have all the endurance and patience you need. May you be filled with joy, always thanking the Father. He has enabled you to share in the inheritance that belongs to his people, who live in the light. For he has rescued us from the kingdom of darkness and transferred us into the Kingdom of his dear Son, who purchased our freedom and forgave our sins.

Colossians 1:11–14

When Jesus' broken body hung on that cross, blood dripped off of His body, fell to the ground, and *shook the earth*. The sky turned dark. The veil tore in two. Hell shuddered. The demons weren't prepared for such a great unearthing. They thought they'd won. But they'd be wrong.

The reason Jesus served Communion before He went to the cross is because we tend to forget the wonder-working, earth-shaking nature of Christ's sacrifice. He doesn't ask us to remember His suffering so we'll continually feel bad about what He endured. On the contrary, Jesus asks us to remember the price He paid so we'll more firmly grasp how free, cherished, and saved we really are! He purchased our freedom with His precious blood.

You're not free and forgiven only when you feel free or perform well. *If the Son sets you free, you are free indeed.*[3]

Prepare Him Room

Precious Jesus, I confess it's difficult for me to spend time pondering Your crucifixion. Yet it's that very act that made us daughters and sons! You boldly and bravely endured unimaginable scorn and shame, suffering and pain, because we were on Your mind. I was on Your mind. You saved me. You saved me! Help me to grasp the miracle of this news. We celebrate Christmas because You broke through the cosmos, came to earth, and set the redemption of mankind into motion. This is the bravest love story ever told! I worship You this day! I remember You this day! And pause to say thank You for all of the ways You've already changed me! I am rich beyond measure and loved beyond imagination. I open my hands and ask for a fresh revelation of Your sacrifice today. May it ground me more deeply in the kingdom that I might be more assured of my place in Your heart. Thank you, Lord. Amen.

Look Up

Fast from an earthbound mind-set today. Pause and ponder your own redemption and transformation. Consider the miraculous power at work within you even now. Give yourself some time and space to consider the miracle of your story.

Day 24

LIVE THE PROMISED LIFE

Today's Reading: Luke 24

OTHER PASSAGES TO PONDER

Again, he said, "Peace be with you. As the Father has sent me, so I am sending you." Then he breathed on them and said, "Receive the Holy Spirit." —John 20:21–22

After saying this, he was taken up into a cloud while they were watching, and they could no longer see him. As they strained to see him rising into heaven, two white-robed men suddenly stood among them. "Men of Galilee," they said, "why are you standing here staring into heaven? Jesus has been taken from you into heaven, but someday he will return from heaven in the same way you saw him go!" —Acts 1:9–11

If you woke each morning and your heart leapt with hope, knowing that the renewal of all things was just around the corner—might even come today—you would be one happy person. If you knew in every fiber of your being that nothing is lost, that everything will be restored to you and then some, you would be armored against discouragement and despair. If your heart's imagination were filled with rich expectations of all the goodness coming to you, your confidence would be contagious; you would be unstoppable, revolutionary. —John Eldredge[1]

Today brings us to the last day of our Advent journey. I pray it's been a rich pilgrimage for you. Before we wrap up our time together, let's circle back for a moment to the beginning of the story. The angel Gabriel appeared to young Mary and proclaimed, "Greetings, favored woman! The Lord is with you!"

It's interesting how, whenever angels appear in Scripture, fear and terror tend to follow. I imagine the glow, the power, and the earthly phenomena are enough to make anybody tremble and quake. At first, Mary felt fear, but then she settled into the idea that the Lord God Almighty was about to enter the world through her. Wow.

God's call on Mary's life was certainly not an easy one. Yet she'd come to know a love that was out of this world and that would change her (and the multitudes) forever. Even so, consider the cultural norms of that time. Mary was a virgin, pledged to marry Joseph, who was a righteous man. One day, unexpectedly, an angel from heaven interrupts her plans and tells her she's about to become pregnant without physically knowing a man. Surely her mind raced at the implications of it all. Just as there are gossips in our day, there were gossips in Mary's day. Worse yet, if religious leaders didn't believe her, she could be put to death for such a crime. But the long-awaited prophecy was about to be fulfilled. The Savior of the world was about to enter the world through her womb. Exciting on one hand. Terrifying on the other. Mary's response to the angel? "I am the Lord's servant. May everything you have said about me come true."

Mary had a relationship with God. She lived with a certain sense of expectancy. How else do you explain her heart tremblinge one moment and humbly submitting the next? Most people would need a few months to think about such a proposition. Not Mary. She went from terror to trust in a matter of moments. Imagine the fears she had to confront, the looks she had to endure, and the questions that ran through her mind, all while she leaned into God's redemptive plan for her and for the world.

Mary should have been stoned for her "sins," but she was spared. She should have been publicly shunned by Joseph, but he embraced her instead. Even though there were social customs that opposed Mary, there were heavenly realities that endorsed her. Mary trusted God, defied the odds, and lived out her God-appointed call.

Let's revisit this powerful passage from Luke chapter two (and make note once again how when an angel appears, man trembles):

> That night there were shepherds staying in the fields nearby, guarding their flocks of sheep. Suddenly, an angel of the Lord appeared among them, and the radiance of the Lord's glory surrounded them. They were terrified, but the angel reassured them. "Don't be afraid!" he said. "I bring you good news that will bring great joy to all people. The Savior—yes, the Messiah, the Lord—has been born today in Bethlehem, the city of David! And you will recognize him by this sign: You will find a baby wrapped snugly in strips of cloth, lying in a manger."
>
> Suddenly, the angel was joined by a vast host of others— the armies of heaven—praising God and saying,
>
> > "Glory to God in highest heaven, and peace on earth to those with whom God is pleased."
>
> Luke 2:8–14

Picture the following scenes, if you will: Shepherds overwhelmed by an encounter with heaven and the message of good news for all people. Mary holds Jesus close to her breast, nurses Him, and begs God for courage to raise Him. Watch Mary giggle as Jesus learns to walk and talk. Her momma heart bursts with affection for her son, who is also God's Son. Imagine how startled she must have been when the caravan left town but Jesus stayed behind and decided to teach at the temple, even though He was still a young boy. Envision her vulnerability once Jesus left home, went public, and began a ministry that would last only a few short years. Try to imagine her indescribable heartbreak as she watched cruel, jealous religious leaders murder her beautiful Son, because they were jealous of and threatened by Him. Mary, more than anyone, knew Jesus' heart and how pure it was. She'd watched as He stood up for the oppressed, healed the sick, cared for the weak. She knew—without a doubt—that there was no guile in Him. He was innocent. Didn't deserve such vile treatment. Yet He Himself predicted this all would happen.

———

This brings us to the final chapter in the gospel of Luke. Jesus had died on the cross. The community grieved the loss of a man who had turned the world upside down. Let's read on (and once again, note the power that surrounded the angels and the terror it caused in the hearts of the women; but notice too how in a matter of moments, they settled in and responded to the message delivered to them):

> But very early on Sunday morning the women went to the tomb, taking the spices they had prepared. They found that the stone had been rolled away from the entrance. So they went in, but they didn't find the body of the Lord Jesus. As

they stood there puzzled, two men suddenly appeared to them, clothed in dazzling robes.

The women were terrified and bowed with their faces to the ground. Then the men asked, "Why are you looking among the dead for someone who is alive? He isn't here! He is risen from the dead! Remember what he told you back in Galilee, that the Son of Man must be betrayed into the hands of sinful men and be crucified, and that he would rise again on the third day."

Then they remembered that he had said this. So they rushed back from the tomb to tell his eleven disciples—and everyone else—what had happened.

Luke 24:1–9

So why all the focus on the angels, the wonder, and the ability to settle into a magnificent, unknown, God-given call? Because *just* as the Father sent His Son, so the Son sends *you.* Jesus left the earth so that the Holy Spirit could come and fill us afresh with the very power of heaven. You are called to live a life that goes way beyond your skill set, passions, and experience. Though God uses all of those things—wonderfully so—He invites you to so much more than your limited assets can contain. The very power that raised Christ from the grave is alive, accessible, and at work within you.

Something often happens to us at Christmastime. We settle into what we know. We love our comforts and we love our plan. Nothing wrong with that. But do not let this sacred holiday pass you by without asking, appealing to the God of angel armies for a fresh perspective on your life. There's a mystery to His ways. There are parts of your story that He won't reveal until you're upon them in the moment. Like there were for Mary, there'll be challenges that leave you breathless. But in the process, you'll get to know the Love that has changed the world. As you cultivate a life of intimacy with God and an expectancy around His ways, you'll find yourself more ready to settle into His plan, even if you don't understand it.

Dare to look up this holiday season and ask for something new. Ask the Lord Himself to reveal a fresh revelation of His love, one that leaves you undone and renewed, all at the same time. Ask Him for new levels of awe and wonder that you might dare to go forward into your future, unafraid, full of hope. Train your thoughts to excitedly think about eternity because of the astonishing goodness that awaits you on the other side. May this holiday season launch you into your next season with the full assurance that you are one of God's dear children, covered, cared for, and called. And His plans for you are only and always good.

> *As you cultivate a life of intimacy with God and an expectancy around His ways, you'll find yourself more ready to settle into His plan, even if you don't understand it.*

I pray that our time together has helped your roots go down deep into the soil of God's marvelous love. I pray His Word becomes one of your most treasured possessions. And I pray that His love compels you to live the impossible life that Jesus made possible for you. Snuggle up with a cup of Christmas tea this season, and remember, I'll be praying for you. A most blessed and merry Christmas to you.

PREPARE HIM ROOM

King Jesus, how I love You! I submit to Your rule and reign in my life. I ask You to grant me a fresh revelation of Your unfathomable love. Awaken my senses to Your very real presence in my life. I give You my full-hearted yes. I will follow where You lead. Like Mary, I say, "May everything You've said about me come true." I know this: You've said I'm loved, called, chosen, and part of the royal family. My name is registered in heaven. Help me to live the life You've promised me. You are the reason I live. And regardless of how the world commercializes this time of year, I know that You're the reason for this season. Help me to live like the kingdom woman You've made me to be. Amen.

LOOK UP

Fast from familiarity. Stay astonished. Embrace wonder. You've countless reasons to stand in awe this holiday season. So stand, bow, sing, and rejoice. Our Savior has come to earth, and soon He'll return to take us home.

ACKNOWLEDGMENTS

Deepest thanks to my acquisitions editor and friend Andy McGuire. I thank God for your friendship, wise counsel, and thoughtful feedback.

Thanks too to the marketing team at Bethany House Publishers. So grateful for your hard work and servant hearts.

Much gratitude to the cover design department (who so rarely get acknowledged, it seems). You are brilliant and amazing. Thank you!

Huge appreciation for my team at Faith Radio. You're always so gracious and patient with me when I'm on deadline. I absolutely LOVE serving with you!

Over-the-moon love to my sons, daughters-in-love, and grandchildren. You are my greatest treasures.

Love and affection to my dear husband, best friend, and powerful partner in ministry. I can't imagine doing this journey without you.

Worship, awe, and adoration for my King Jesus. I pray the words in this book reflect Your heart for a world in need. We're waiting for You.

NOTES

Day 1: Embrace Expectancy

1. Daniel Darling, *The Characters of Christmas: The Unlikely People Caught Up in the Story of Jesus* (Chicago: Moody Publishers, 2019), 45, emphasis mine.

Day 2: The Savior of the World

1. Asheritah Ciuciu, *Unwrapping the Names of Jesus: An Advent Devotional* (Chicago: Moody Publishers, 2017), 31.

2. Jennifer Kennedy Dean, *Secrets Jesus Shared: Kingdom Insights Revealed through the Parables* (Birmingham, AL: New Hope Publishers, 2007), 47.

3. See Revelation 3:20.

4. Ciuciu, *Unwrapping the Names*, 30–31.

Day 3: Prepare the Way

1. John Fischer, *12 Steps for a Recovering Pharisee (like me): Finding Grace to Live Unmasked* (Bloomington, MN: Bethany House, 2000), 58.

Day 5: Addition, Subtraction, and Multiplication

1. Max Lucado, *God Came Near: God's Perfect Gift* (Nashville: Thomas Nelson, 2004), 4.

2. Paraphrase of Luke 5:1–4.

Day 6: The Kingdom Is Yours

1. Jen Pollock Michel, *Surprised by Paradox: The Promise of And in an Either-Or World* (Downers Grove, IL: IVP Books, 2019), 71.

2. See Acts 17:25.
3. See Romans 8:1.
4. See Luke 6:35–36.

Day 7: Encountering Jesus

1. Bo Stern, *When Holidays Hurt: Finding Hidden Hope Amid Pain and Loss* (Nashville: Thomas Nelson, 2014), 28.
2. See Revelation 19:9.
3. Alicia Britt Chole, *Anonymous: Jesus' Hidden Years . . . and Yours* (Nashville: Thomas Nelson, 2006), 44.

Day 8: The Gift of Presence and Listening

1. Mark Batterson, *Whisper: How to Hear the Voice of God* (Colorado Springs: Multnomah, 2017), 2–3.

Day 9: A Physical and Spiritual Kingdom

1. *Life Application Study Bible: New Living Translation* (Carol Stream, IL: Tyndale House, 2007), 212, Luke 9:2 study note, emphasis mine.
2. Jim Martin with International Justice Mission said this on my show one day: "Maybe your problems aren't too big; they're too small."

Day 10: Marvel

1. Max Lucado, *You Are Never Alone: Trust in the Miracle of God's Presence and Power* (Nashville: Thomas Nelson, 2020), 100–101.

Day 11: Ask, Don't Demand

1. Mark Batterson, *Draw the Circle: The 40 Day Prayer Challenge* (Grand Rapids, MI: Zondervan, 2012), 119.
2. Phillips Brooks, *Forty Thousand Quotations: Prose and Poetical*, comp. Charles Noel Douglas (New York: Halcyon House, 1917), Bartleby.com, 2012, www.bartleby.com/348/authors/68.html.
3. My paraphrase of Philippians 4:6–7.
4. See Psalm 138:6.
5. See Matthew 5:3 NIV.
6. See Luke 11:34.

Day 12: Pride and Presentation

1. Holley Gerth, *Fiercehearted: Live Fully, Love Bravely* (Grand Rapids, MI: Revell, 2017), 111.

Day 13: Contend for the Faith

1. *Life Application Study Bible: New Living Translation* (Carol Stream, IL: Tyndale House, 2007), 2699, study note.

2. Entry for Strong's #75, Thayer's definition, "Bible Lexicons," Study Light.org, accessed December 8, 2020, https://www.studylight.org/lexicons /greek/75.html.

Day 14: See the Story

1. John Eldredge, *Get Your Life Back: Everyday Practices for a World Gone Mad* (Nashville: Thomas Nelson, 2020), 71.

2. See Matthew 5:12.

3. My friend Jodi said this to me over lunch one day.

Day 15: Jesus Pursues the Wanderer

1. C. S. Lewis, as spoken by Queen Lucy in *The Last Battle* (New York: HarperCollins, 1956), 102.

2. Paraphrased from *Life Application Study Bible: New Living Translation* (Carol Stream, IL: Tyndale House, 2004), 2238, study note on Luke 15:8–10.

Day 16: Shrewd, Not Scrooge

1. Charles Dickens, describing the "new" Scrooge, *A Christmas Carol and Other Christmas Writings* (New York: Penguin Books, 2003), 115.

Day 17: Live like Jesus

1. Jon Tyson, *Beautiful Resistance: The Joy of Conviction in a Culture of Compromise* (Colorado Springs: Multnomah, 2020), 167.

Day 18: Do You Know Him?

1. S. M. Lockridge, "That's My King," audio sermon, accessed December 8, 2020, https://www.audiosermon.net/video-sermons/551-all -media/sermons/dr-s-m-lockridge/286-that-s-my-king-full-sermon-dr -s-m-lockridge.

2. Check out *Your Powerful Prayers*, if you're interested.

3. Susie Larson, *Your Powerful Prayers: Reaching the Heart of God with a Bold and Humble Faith* (Bloomington, MN: Bethany House, 2016), 174.

4. Entry for Strong's #4102, Thayer's definition, "Bible Lexicons," StudyLight.org, accessed December 8, 2020, https://www.studylight.org/lexicons/greek/4102.html.

Day 19: An Unexpected Savior

1. Alicia Britt Chole, *40 Days of Decrease: A Different Kind of Hunger. A Different Kind of Fast.* (Nashville: Thomas Nelson, 2016), 67.

Day 20: Live, Don't Watch

1. Holley Gerth, *Fiercehearted: Live Fully, Love Bravely* (Grand Rapids, MI: Revell, 2017), 25.

2. Luke 20:20–21.

Day 21: Discern the Times

1. Warren W. Wiersbe, *The Wiersbe Bible Commentary: New Testament* (Colorado Springs: David C. Cook, 2007), 212.

2. Wiersbe, *The Wiersbe Bible Commentary*, 209.

Day 22: Communion

1. Susie Larson, *The Uncommon Woman: Making an Ordinary Life Extraordinary* (Chicago: Moody Publishers, 2008), 135.

2. Larson, *The Uncommon Woman*, 135.

Day 23: Death Defeated!

1. Charles Martin, *What If It's True?: A Storyteller's Journey with Jesus* (Nashville: Thomas Nelson, 2019), 113.

2. See 2 Corinthians 9:6–13.

3. See John 8:36.

Day 24: Live the Promised Life

1. John Eldredge, *All Things New: Heaven, Earth, and the Restoration of Everything You Love* (Nashville: Thomas Nelson, 2017), 200.

Susie Larson is a popular talk-radio host, national speaker, and author of sixteen books. Susie has twice been voted a top-ten finalist for the John C. Maxwell Transformational Leadership Award. This award recognizes people who go beyond themselves to make a positive impact in the lives of others. Some of her previous books include *Prevail*, *Fully Alive*, *Your Beautiful Purpose*, *Your Powerful Prayers*, *Growing Grateful Kids*, and *The Uncommon Woman*. Susie has been married to her dear husband, Kevin, since 1985, and together they have three wonderful sons, three beautiful daughters-in-law, two precious grandchildren, and one adorable pit bull named Memphis. Susie's passion is to see people everywhere awakened to the value of their soul, the depth of God's love, and the height of their calling in Christ Jesus.

More from Susie Larson

Everything God asks of us is for our good and His glory. But that doesn't mean life is easy, and sometimes we need to be reminded of God's power over all we face. In this inspiring devotional, Susie Larson offers 365 days' worth of opportunities for you to strengthen your faith while finding a new level of freedom and redemption.

Prevail

In this eye-opening book, Susie Larson shows how intertwined our emotional, spiritual, and physical health is. For true healing to occur, it must happen holistically—mind, body, and spirit. Providing a fresh vision of what a flourishing life is, Susie shares practical, biblical ways to walk the path of healing and wholeness in every area of life.

Fully Alive